Keto
IN FIVE

120 *low-carb* recipes

Up to **5** net carbs, **5** ingredients & **5** easy steps for every recipe

Vicky Ushakova and Rami Abramov

Contents

Dessert in Five

Disclaimer

Tasteaholics, Inc. is not a medical company or organization. Our books provide information in respect to healthy eating, nutrition and recipes and are intended for informational purposes only. We are not nutritionists or doctors and the information in this book and our website is not meant to be given as medical advice. We are two people sharing our success strategies and resources and encouraging you to do further research to see if they'll work for you too. Before starting any diet, you should always consult with your physician to rule out any health issues that could arise. Safety first, results second. Do not disregard professional medical advice or delay in seeking it because of this book.

About This Book

This book was designed as a guide to help you kick start your ketogenic diet so you can lose weight, become healthy and have high energy levels every day.

Inside this book, you'll find the basics of the ketogenic diet, useful tips and delicious breakfast, lunch, dinner & dessert recipes.

Each recipe is only 5 grams of net carbs or fewer and can be made with just 5 ingredients! There's nothing better than that.

Eating low-carb doesn't require cutting out wholesome, nutritious foods or sacrificing taste — ever. We hand selected each ingredient to not only serve a delicious purpose but provide nutritious benefits.

Enjoy 120 delicious and easy low-carb recipes including pancakes, waffles, French crepes, creamy chowders, tacos, mouthwatering casseroles, heavenly steaks, gourmet-style seafood, chocolate soufflés, strawberry cheesecakes & much more that'll keep you full and excited every day of the month.

Let's get started!

4

Keto 101

What Is Keto?

The Ketogenic Diet

The ketogenic (or keto) diet is a low-carbohydrate, high-fat diet. Maintaining this diet is a great tool for weight loss. More importantly, according to an increasing number of studies, it reduces risk factors for diabetes, heart diseases, stroke, Alzheimer's, epilepsy, and more.[1-6]

On the keto diet, your body enters a metabolic state called ketosis. While in ketosis your body is using ketone bodies for energy instead of glucose. Ketone bodies are derived from fat and are a much more stable, steady source of energy than glucose, which is derived from carbohydrates.

Entering ketosis usually takes anywhere from 3 days to a week. Once you're in ketosis, you'll be using fat for energy, instead of carbs. This includes the fat you eat and stored body fat.

While eating low-carb, you'll lose weight easier, feel satiated longer and enjoy consistent energy levels throughout your day.

Testing for Ketosis

You can test yourself to see whether you've entered ketosis just a few days after you've begun the keto diet! Use a *ketone urine test strip* and it will tell you the level of ketone bodies in your urine. If the concentration is high enough and the test strip shows any hue of purple, you've successfully entered ketosis!

The strips take only a few seconds to show results and are the fastest and most affordable way to check whether you're in ketosis.

Visit tasteaholics.com/strips and get a bottle of 100 test strips.

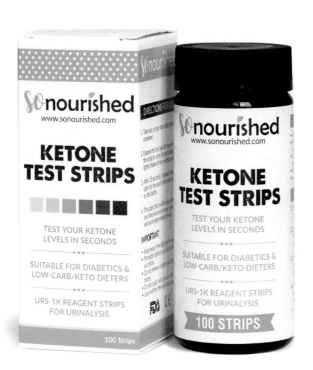

The Truth About Fat

You may be thinking, "but eating a lot of fat is bad!" The truth is, dozens of studies and meta studies with over 900,000 subjects have arrived at similar conclusions: eating saturated and monounsaturated fats have no effects on heart disease risks.[7,8]

Most fats are good and are essential to our health. Fats (fatty acids) and protein (amino acids) are essential for survival.

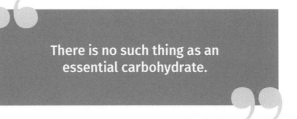

> There is no such thing as an essential carbohydrate.

Fats are the most efficient form of energy and each gram contains more than double the energy in a gram of protein or carbohydrates (more on that later).

The keto diet promotes eating fresh, whole foods like meat, fish, veggies, and healthy fats and oils as well as greatly reducing processed and chemically treated foods the Standard American Diet (SAD) has so long encouraged.

It's a diet that you can sustain long-term and enjoy. What's not to enjoy about bacon and eggs in the morning?

Calories & Macronutrients

How Calories Work

A calorie is a unit of energy. When something contains 100 calories, it describes how much energy your body could get from consuming it. Calorie consumption dictates weight gain/loss.

If you burn an average of 1,800 calories and eat 2,000 calories per day, you will gain weight.

If you do light exercise that burns an extra 300 calories per day, you'll burn 2,100 calories per day, putting you at a deficit of 100 calories. Simply by eating at a deficit, you will lose weight because your body will tap into stored resources for the remaining energy it needs.

That being said, it's important to get the right balance of macronutrients every day so your body has the energy it needs.

tasteaholics.com/calculator

What Are Macronutrients?

Macronutrients (macros) are molecules that our bodies use to create energy for themselves — primarily fat, protein and carbs. They are found in all food and are measured in grams (g) on nutrition labels.

* **Fat** provides 9 calories per gram

* **Protein** provides 4 calories per gram

* **Carbs** provide 4 calories per gram

Learn more at tasteaholics.com/macros.

Net Carbs

Most low-carb recipes write net carbs when displaying their macros. Net carbs are total carbs minus dietary fiber and sugar alcohols. Our bodies can't break them down into glucose so they don't count toward your total carb count.

Note: *Dietary fiber can be listed as soluble or insoluble.*

How Much Should You Eat?

On a keto diet, about 65 to 75 percent of the calories you consume daily should come from fat. About 20 to 30 percent should come from protein. The remaining 5 percent or so should come from carbohydrates.

Use our keto calculator to figure out exactly how many calories and macros you should be eating every day!

It will ask for basic information including your weight, activity levels and goals and instantly provide you with the total calories and grams of fat, protein and carbs that you should be eating each day.

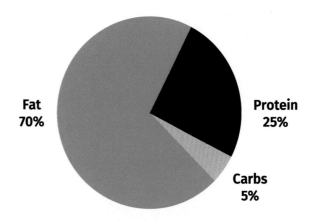

Note: *The calculator should be used as a general guideline. The results are based on your inputs and variables such as body fat percentage and basal metabolic rate are difficult to estimate correctly.*

A Nutritional Revolution

Carbs: What Exactly Are They?

Carbohydrates (carbs) are found in things like starches, grains and foods high in sugar. This includes, but isn't limited to, bread, flour, rice, pasta, beans, potatoes, sugar, syrup, cereals, fruits, bagels and soda.

Carbs are broken down into glucose (a type of sugar) in our bodies for energy. Eating any kinds of carbs spikes blood sugar levels. The spike may happen faster or slower depending on the type of carb (based on the glycemic index), but the spike will still happen.

Blood sugar spikes cause strong insulin releases to combat the spikes. Constant insulin releases result in fat storage and insulin resistance. After many years, this cycle can lead to prediabetes, metabolic syndrome and even type 2 diabetes.[9]

In a world full of sugar, cereal, pasta, burgers, French fries and large sodas, you can see how carbs can easily be overconsumed.

Where We Are Today

According to the 2014 report by the Centers for Disease Control and Prevention (CDC), more than 1 in 3 adults in the U.S. (86 million people) have prediabetes, a condition in which blood glucose is always high and commonly leads to type 2 diabetes and many other medical problems.[10]

Today, almost 1 in 10 people in the U.S. have type 2 diabetes compared to almost 1 in 40 in 1980.

Fat has been blamed as the bad guy and carbohydrates have been considered crucial and healthy. Companies have been creating low-fat and fat-free, chemical-laden alternatives of nearly every type of fc yet diabetes and heart di still increasing.

Fat Is Making a Comeback

Hundreds of studies have been conducted in the past ten years which have been corroborating the same data: that eating healthy fats is not detrimental to health and is, in fact, more beneficial than eating a diet high in carbohydrates.

We're starting to understand that carbs in large quantities are much more harmful than previously thought, while most fats are healthy and essential.

The nutritional landscape is changing. Low-carb and similar dietary groups are growing and a nutritional revolution is beginning. We are beginning to realize the detrimental effects of our relationship with excess sugar and carbs.

The Basics: Benefits of Going Keto

Long-Term Benefits

Studies consistently show that those who eat a low-carb, high-fat diet rather than a high-carb, low-fat diet:

- Lose more weight and body fat[11–17]

- Have better levels of good cholesterol (HDL and large LDL)[18,19]

- Have reduced blood sugar and insulin resistance (commonly reversing prediabetes and type 2 diabetes)[20,21]

- Experience a decrease in appetite[22]

- Have reduced triglyceride levels (fat molecules in the blood that cause heart disease)[19,23]

- Have significant reductions in blood pressure, leading to a reduction in heart disease and stroke[24]

Day-To-Day Benefits

The keto diet doesn't only provide long-term benefits! When you're on keto, you can expect to:

- Lose body fat

- Have stable energy levels during the day

- Stay satiated after meals longer, with less snacking and overeating

Longer satiation and consistent energy levels are due to the majority of calories coming from fat, which is slower to digest and calorically denser.

Eating low-carb also eliminates blood glucose spikes and crashes. You won't have sudden blood sugar drops leaving you feeling weak and disoriented.

Entering Ketosis

The keto diet's main goal is to keep you in nutritional ketosis all the time. If you're just getting started with your keto diet, you should eat up to 25 grams of carbs per day.

Once you're in ketosis for long enough (about 4 to 8 weeks), you become keto-adapted, or fat-adapted. This is when your glycogen stores in muscles and liver are depleted, you carry less water weight, muscle endurance increases and your overall energy levels are higher.

Once keto-adapted, you can usually eat ≈50 grams of net carbs a day to maintain ketosis.

Type 1 Diabetes & Ketoacidosis

If you have type 1 diabetes, consult with your doctor before starting a keto diet. Diabetic ketoacidosis (DKA) is a dangerous condition that can occur if you have type 1 diabetes due to a shortage of insulin.

Steering Clear of the Keto Flu

What Is the Keto Flu?

The keto flu happens commonly to keto dieters due to low levels of sodium and electrolytes and has flu-like symptoms including:

- Fatigue
- Headaches
- Cough
- Sniffles
- Irritability
- Nausea

It's important to note that this isn't the real flu! It's called keto flu due to similar symptoms but it is not at all contagious and doesn't actually involve a virus.

Why Does It Happen?

The main cause of keto flu is your body lacking electrolytes, especially sodium. When starting keto, you cut out lots of processed foods and eat more whole, natural foods. Although this is great, it causes a sudden drop in sodium intake.

> **The keto flu can be avoided by consuming enough electrolytes, especially sodium.**

In addition, reducing carbs reduces insulin levels, which reduces sodium stored by kidneys.[25]

Between your reduced sodium intake and stored sodium flushed by your kidneys, you end up being low on sodium and other electrolytes.

Ending the Keto Flu

The best way to avoid or end the keto flu is to add more sodium and electrolytes to your diet. Here are the most effective (and tasty) ways to get more sodium:

- Adding more salt to your food
- Drinking soup broth
- Eating plenty of salty foods like bacon and pickled vegetables

Try to eat more sodium as you start the keto diet to prevent the keto flu entirely. If you do catch it, just remember that it'll go away quickly and you'll emerge a fat-burning machine!

Note: *For more information about the keto flu, read our full guide at* tasteaholics.com/keto-flu.

Starting Keto

Part 1 — Out with the Old

Having tempting, unhealthy foods in your home is one of the biggest reasons for failure when starting any diet.

To maximize your chances of success, you need to remove as many triggers as you can. This crucial step will help prevent moments of weakness from ruining all your hard work.

If you aren't living alone, make sure to discuss with your family or housemates before throwing anything out. If some items are simply not yours to throw out, try to compromise and agree on a special location so you can keep them out of sight and out of mind.

Once your home is free of temptation, eating low-carb is far less difficult and success is that much easier.

Starches and Grains

Get rid of all cereal, pasta, bread, rice, potatoes, corn, oats, quinoa, flour, bagels, rolls, croissants and wraps.

All Sugary Things

Throw away and forget all refined sugar, fruit juices, desserts, fountain drinks, milk chocolate, pastries, candy bars, etc.

Legumes

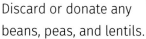

Discard or donate any beans, peas, and lentils.

Vegetable & Seed Oils

Stop using any vegetable oils and seed oils like sunflower, safflower, soybean, canola, corn and grapeseed oil. Get rid of trans fats like margarine.

Read Nutrition Labels

Check the nutrition labels on all your products to see if they're high in carbs. There are hidden carbs in the unlikeliest of places (like ketchup and canned soups). Try to avoid buying products with dozens of incomprehensible ingredients. Less is usually healthier.

For example:

> Deli ham can have 2 or 3 grams of sugar per slice as well as many added preservatives and nitrites!

Always check the serving sizes against the carb counts. Manufacturers can sometimes recommend inconceivably small serving sizes to seemingly reduce calorie and carb numbers.

At first glance, something may be low in carbs, but a quick comparison to the serving size can reveal the product is mostly sugar. Be diligent!

Nutrition Facts

Serving Size 1 Cup (53g/1.9 oz.)
Servings Per Container About 8

Amount Per Serving

Calories 190	Calories from Fat 25

	% Daily Value*
Total Fat 3g	5%
Saturated Fat 0g	0%
Trans Fat 0g	
Cholesterol 0mg	0%
Sodium 100mg	4%
Potassium 300mg	9%
Total Carbohydrate 37g	12%
Dietary Fiber 8g	32%
Soluble Fiber	
Insoluble Fibe	
Sugars 13g	
Protein 9g	14%

Vitamin A 0%		C 0%

Part 2 – In with the New!

Now that you've cleaned out everything you don't need, it's time to restock your pantry and fridge with delicious and wholesome, keto-friendly foods that will help you lose weight, become healthier, and feel amazing!

General Products to Have

With these basics in your home, you'll always be ready to make healthy, keto-friendly meals.

- Lots of water, coffee, and unsweetened tea
- Stevia and erythritol (sweeteners)
- Condiments like mayonnaise, mustard, pesto, and sriracha
- Broths (beef, chicken, bone)
- Pickles and other fermented foods
- Seeds and nuts (chia seeds, flaxseeds, pecans, almonds, walnuts, macadamias, etc.)

Meat, Fish & Eggs

Just about every type of fresh meat and fish is good for keto including beef, chicken, lamb, pork, salmon, tuna, etc. Eat grass-fed and/or organic meat and wild-caught fish whenever possible.

Eat as many eggs as you like, preferably organic from free-range chickens.

Vegetables

Eat plenty of non-starchy veggies including asparagus, mushrooms, broccoli, cucumber, lettuce, onions, peppers, cauliflower, tomatoes, garlic, Brussels sprouts and zucchini.

Dairy

You can eat full-fat dairy like sour cream, heavy (whipping) cream, butter, cheeses and unsweetened yogurt.

Although not dairy, unsweetened almond milk and coconut milk are both good milk substitutes.

Stay away from regular milk, skim milk and sweetened yogurts because they contain a lot of sugar. Avoid all fat-free and low-fat dairy products.

Oils and Fats

Olive oil, avocado oil, butter and bacon fat are great for cooking and consuming. Avocado oil is best for searing due to its very high smoke point (520°F).

Fruits

Berries like strawberries, blueberries, raspberries, etc. are allowed in small amounts. Avocados are great because they're low-carb and very high in fat!

Notes

- We use large eggs in all our recipes. If yours are a different size, know that this will affect the nutrition slightly.

- The sugar-free, low-carb protein powder we use is *Isopure* Vanilla and *Isopure* Chocolate.

- Try to find the most natural peanut and almond butter brands you can. The ingredients listed should be, at most, 2 ingredients long.

- If you don't have stevia, feel free to substitute your favorite sugar-free sweetener like erythritol, xylitol, Splenda, etc. Add a little at a time and work your way up to taste.

  - You can order erythritol online by visiting tasteaholics.com/erythritol.

- The mozzarella cheese in each recipe is a low-moisture, part-skim, shredded mozzarella cheese; not fresh mozzarella.

- If you see the abbreviation "SF" it is short for "sugar-free".

  - For example, "SF Maple Syrup" means we used *Walden Farms* or *Sukrin Gold* syrup, both of which are sugar-free brands.

- If you're not a fan of spicy foods, feel free to leave out ingredients like jalapeño peppers, hot sauce, red pepper flakes, etc.

- The marinara sauce we use in all our recipes is of the brand *Rao's Homemade Sauces*. They are a low-sugar or no sugar added tomato sauce maker which can be found in many supermarkets. You can also choose to make your own from scratch or use any low-sugar tomato sauce you have on hand.

- A food scale is a must if you're counting calories and macros. Many of our ingredients are listed by weight to provide accurate nutritional data.

Low-Carb Friendly Seasonings

The following herbs and spices may be used in any of our recipes should you wish to add them.

They are all low-carb though we suggest limiting them to under a tablespoon to stay within your daily goals. It's more than enough to add their delicious flavors to your dishes without putting you over your carb limit!

☐ Salt
☐ Pepper
☐ Paprika
☐ Cayenne
☐ Thyme
☐ Basil
☐ Oregano
☐ Parsley
☐ Rosemary
☐ Tarragon
☐ Sage
☐ Cumin
☐ Red pepper flakes
☐ Sesame seeds

How to Make Cloud Buns

Whether you call them Oopsie Rolls, Cloud Bread or Cloud Buns, you'll see them being used in a few of our breakfast recipes. They can be made using only 3 ingredients so they're perfect for our purposes. We recommend making a batch the night before or on Sunday to have for the week.

Store them in an air-tight container in the refrigerator with some parchment paper in between each bun for up to a week. You can also freeze them in a single layer on a baking sheet, then transfer into a large Ziploc bag and store for up to 2 months.

Nutrition per Cloud Bun

50 calories | Makes 10–12 Cloud Buns

- 4 grams of fat
- 2.5 grams of protein
- 0.7 grams of carbs

🕐 **Prep Time: 10 mins | Cook Time: 30 mins**

Ingredients

- 3 large eggs
- 3 oz. cream cheese, cubed
- ⅛ tsp. cream of tartar or ⅛ tsp. baking powder

Instructions

1. Preheat the oven to 300°F.
2. Separate the eggs into two mixing bowls.
3. Beat the egg whites with a clean, electric hand mixer until foamy.
4. Add cream of tartar (or baking powder) and beat until opaque and shiny.
5. Beat the cream cheese and egg yolks until well combined and pale in color.
6. Fold the egg whites into the egg yolk mixture very gently.
7. Spoon ¼ cup at a time onto a parchment paper-lined baking sheet about 1–2 inches apart and bake for 30 minutes.
8. Let cool completely before removing and enjoying.

Breakfast IN FIVE

---

30 *low-carb* breakfasts

Up to **5** net carbs, **5** ingredients & **5** easy steps for every recipe

Blueberry Almond Pancakes

Low sugar, gluten-free and dairy-free pancakes that are incredibly easy to make. They taste and feel so close to the real thing!

Nutrition

500 calories per serving | Makes 2 servings

| 42 grams of fat
| 20 grams of protein
| 5 grams of net carbs

Ingredients

- 1 cup almond flour
- 3 large eggs
- 1 ½ tsp. baking powder
- 50 grams frozen blueberries
- 2 tbsp. unsalted butter

Instructions

1. Combine almond flour, eggs, baking powder and a pinch of salt. Whisk until creamy. Thin out the batter with 1–2 tablespoons of water.
2. Heat a griddle and pour the batter to make 6, 5-inch pancakes. Add blueberries to each one.
3. Cook until you see bubbles forming on top, flip and cook again until golden brown.
4. Serve with butter and enjoy!

Avocado Cloud Toast

You, too, can have toast in the mornings! Topped with tangy mayo, a juicy slice of tomato and creamy avocado! Total perfection.

Nutrition

535 calories per serving | Makes 2 servings

- 52 grams of fat
- 6 grams of protein
- 3 grams of net carbs

⏱ **Prep Time: 5 mins | Cook Time: 0 mins**

Ingredients

- 4 Cloud Buns (see p. 24)
- 8 tbsp. mayonnaise
- 4 large tomato slices
- 1 large avocado
- Salt & pepper to taste

Instructions

1. Prepare the Cloud Buns recipe on page 28 the night before. Toast 4 buns until golden.
2. Open and pit the avocado. Cut it into quarters and slice them lengthwise.
3. Add 2 tablespoons of mayonnaise, a slice of tomato and 1 quarter of the sliced avocado to each toasted cloud bun.
4. Sprinkle with salt and pepper and enjoy!

Maple Pecan Porridge

A good sugar-free maple syrup is great to have around to sweeten low-carb treats — like this warm, filling maple pecan porridge!

Nutrition

390 calories per serving | Makes 2 servings

- 37 grams of fat
- 8 grams of protein
- 5 grams of net carbs

⏱ **Prep Time: 5 mins | Cook Time: 10 mins**

Ingredients

- ¼ cup flaxseed meal
- ¼ cup coconut flour
- ½ tsp. ground cinnamon
- 3 oz. pecans, toasted
- ¼ cup sugar-free maple syrup

Instructions

1. Heat 2 cups of water in a small pot.
2. Once steamy, add flaxseed meal, coconut flour and cinnamon to it. Stir until combined and cook until the whole thing has thickened.
3. Divide into bowls and garnish with whole or chopped toasted pecans.
4. Drizzle with sugar-free maple syrup and enjoy! (see p. 22) for maple syrup recommendations.)

Chorizo Breakfast Bake

These quick little cups of deliciousness will soon become your favorite breakfast recipe! They're savory, warm and quite filling!

Nutrition

418 calories per serving | Makes 2 servings

- 32 grams of fat
- 27 grams of protein
- 3 grams of net carbs

⏱ **Prep Time: 10 mins | Cook Time: 12 mins**

Ingredients

- ¼ red bell pepper, finely chopped
- ¼ green bell pepper, finely chopped
- 80 grams chorizo sausage, cooked
- ½ cup shredded mozzarella (see p. 22)
- 4 large eggs

Instructions

1. Cook the red and green bell peppers in a lightly oiled pan until soft. Slice the chorizo sausage into bite-sized pieces.
2. Lightly grease 4 ramekins and add the peppers, sausage and shredded mozzarella.
3. Crack an egg onto each ramekin and season with salt and pepper.
4. Bake for 12 minutes at 350°F and enjoy!

Loaded Butter Coffee

When you don't have time for a full breakfast but want something that'll keep you full for hours, wake up to this recipe!

Nutrition

490 calories per serving | Makes 1 serving

- 49 grams of fat
- 3 grams of protein
- 1 gram of net carbs

🕐 **Prep Time: 5 mins | Cook Time: 0 mins**

Ingredients

- 1 cup brewed coffee (or 1 shot espresso)
- 1 tbsp. coconut oil
- 1 tbsp. unsalted butter
- ¼ cup heavy cream
- 1 large egg yolk

Instructions

1. Add your favorite brewed coffee or shot of espresso (+ some water) into a blender.
2. Add in the coconut oil, butter, heavy cream and egg yolk.
3. Blend on high until well combined and frothy. Do not skip blending this recipe or the oils will pool up at the top of coffee instead of emulsifying in it.
4. Sweeten if desired and enjoy!

Savory Bacon Pancakes

Not your ordinary pancakes! These bacon pancakes are savory, salty and hearty — perfect for a super filling and unexpected breakfast.

Nutrition

420 calories per serving | Makes 2 servings

32 grams of fat	
25 grams of protein	
4 grams of net carbs	

Ingredients

- 4 oz. cream cheese
- 4 large eggs
- ½ tsp. baking powder
- 6 strips bacon
- 2 stalks green onion, chopped

Instructions

1. Cook the bacon until desired crispiness, then chop it into bits.
2. Add cream cheese, eggs and baking powder into a small blender and blend until smooth.
3. Add the bacon bits and chopped green onion and stir them in.
4. Pour the batter onto a pan or griddle on medium heat and cook until bubbles start to form at the surface, about 3-5 minutes.
5. Flip and cook for another minute. Serve with a sprinkle of green onion and enjoy!

Blueberry Coconut Muffin

Soft, moist and coconutty! This blueberry coconut muffin for one is the perfect recipe to take with you on-the-go or enjoy at home.

Nutrition

375 calories per serving | Makes 1 serving

| | 33 grams of fat
| | 7 grams of protein
| | 5 grams of net carbs

🕐 **Prep Time: 8 mins | Cook Time: 18 mins**

Ingredients

- 2 tbsp. coconut flour
- ½ tsp. baking powder
- 2 tbsp. coconut oil
- 1 large egg
- 15 grams blueberries, fresh or frozen

Instructions

1. Combine the coconut flour and baking powder in a bowl and whisk to get rid of any clumps.
2. Add in coconut oil and an egg and stir until well combined.
3. Fold in a few blueberries and a pinch of salt.
4. Pour into a lightly greased muffin tin and bake at 350°F for about 18 minutes.
5. Let cool completely before enjoying.

Ham, Egg & Cheese 'wich

What could be simpler than a sandwich? Toast up a couple of Cloud Buns and top them with whatever you please!

Nutrition

523 calories per serving | Makes 2 servings

- 44 grams of fat
- 28 grams of protein
- 4 grams of net carbs

🕐 **Prep Time: 5 mins | Cook Time: 5 mins**

Ingredients

- 4 Cloud Buns (see p. 24)
- 4 tbsp. mayonnaise
- 2 large eggs
- 2 slices pepper jack cheese
- 4 oz. black forest ham, sliced

Instructions

1. Prepare the Cloud Buns recipe the night before. Toast 4 buns until golden.
2. Fry the eggs and season with salt and pepper.
3. Add 2 tablespoons of mayonnaise to 2 cloud buns and add a slice of pepper jack cheese.
4. Lay a fried egg over each slice of cheese.
5. Add black forest ham and top with another cloud bun. Enjoy!

Chocolate Chip Waffles

Feel like a kid again with our healthier chocolate chip waffles. They're low-carb, sugar-free & gluten-free. Perfect for any morning!

Nutrition

400 calories per serving | Makes 2 servings

| 26 grams of fat
| 34 grams of protein
| 4.5 grams of net carbs

🕐 **Prep Time: 15 mins | Cook Time: 10 mins**

Ingredients

- 62 grams low-carb protein powder (see p. 22)
- 2 large eggs, separated
- 2 tbsp. melted butter
- 50 grams cacao nibs (or SF chocolate chips)
- Sugar-free maple syrup to taste

Instructions

1. Whisk the egg whites until stiff peaks form.
2. Combine protein powder, egg yolks and melted butter in a mixing bowl and whisk.
3. Gently fold in the egg whites, being very careful not to deflate them, then add cacao nibs (or sugar-free chocolate chips) and a pinch of salt.
4. Grease a waffle iron and cook batter according to the manufacturer's instructions until lightly golden. Do not overcook the waffles!
5. Serve with sugar-free maple syrup and enjoy!

Breakfast Tacos

Breakfast tacos are the perfect Sunday treat for your family! A simple cheese shell is all it takes to have a fun, Spanish-style breakfast.

Nutrition

600 calories per serving | Makes 2 servings

43 grams of fat

46 grams of protein

5 grams of net carbs

⏲ **Prep Time: 10 mins | Cook Time: 15 mins**

Ingredients

- 1 ½ cups shredded mozzarella (see p. 22)
- 6 large eggs
- 4 strips bacon
- ½ avocado, cubed
- 1 roma tomato, chopped

Instructions

1. Add a ¼ cup of shredded mozzarella at a time to a hot pan. Let it melt and brown. Flip and let the other side brown.
2. Gently remove the cheese using a spatula and drape it over a wooden spoon set on a bowl to cool into a taco shape. Repeat for all the cheese.
3. Cook the bacon and chop into bits. Scramble the eggs and season them with salt and pepper.
4. Add bacon bits, eggs, avocado, tomato and a bit more cheese into the shells and enjoy!

Coconut Macadamia Bars

Breakfast bars are a great way to save some time in the mornings. Make a batch and keep them in the fridge at home or work all week!

Nutrition

375 calories per serving | Makes 5 servings

- 38 grams of fat
- 7 grams of protein
- 5 grams of net carbs

⏱ **Prep Time: 10 mins | Passive Time: 12 hrs**

Ingredients

- 60 grams macadamia nuts
- ½ cup almond butter
- ¼ cup coconut oil, melted
- 6 tbsp. unsweetened shredded coconut
- 20 drops liquid stevia

Instructions

1. Pulse the macadamia nuts in a food processor until very fine.
2. Combine almond butter, coconut oil and coconut in a bowl. Add the nuts and stevia.
3. Mix thoroughly and pour the batter into a 9×9" parchment paper-lined baking dish.
4. Refrigerate overnight, slice and enjoy chilled.

Tip: *These bars work wonderfully frozen too!*

Morning Hot Pockets

Imagine the possibilities when you perfect these amazingly versatile hot pockets. You can fill them with just about anything you like!

Nutrition

455 calories per serving | Makes 2 servings

- 38 grams of fat
- 25 grams of protein
- 3 grams of net carbs

🕐 **Prep Time: 20 mins | Cook Time: 20 mins**

Ingredients

- ¾ cup shredded mozzarella (see p. 22)
- ⅓ cup almond flour
- 2 large eggs
- 2 tbsp. unsalted butter
- 3 slices bacon, cooked

Instructions

1. Melt the shredded mozzarella and add in the almond flour. Stir until well combined, microwaving again if necessary. Roll the dough out between 2 sheets of parchment paper until about a ½ cm. thick.
2. Scramble the eggs in the butter and lay them with the cooked bacon slices along the center of the flattened dough.
3. Fold the dough over itself and seal the seam by pinching the edges. Add some holes on top for releasing some steam while baking.
4. Bake, seam down, at 400°F for about 20 minutes or until golden brown and firm and dry to the touch.

Strawberries & Cream Shake

Shakes and smoothies have a very special place in a busy person's life. Our strawberries & cream shake is sweet and light, yet quite filling!

Nutrition

430 calories per serving | Makes 2 servings

- 49 grams of fat
- 3 grams of protein
- 5 grams of net carbs

⏱ **Prep Time: 8 mins | Cook Time: 0 mins**

Ingredients

- 80 grams strawberries
- 1 cup unsweetened almond milk
- 1 cup heavy cream
- ½ tsp. vanilla extract
- 10 drops liquid stevia (optional)

Instructions

1. Rinse and hull the strawberries.
2. Pour the almond milk and heavy cream into a blender.
3. Throw the strawberries in along with the vanilla extract and stevia, if desired.
4. Blend on high until completely combined and creamy.
5. Enjoy!

On-The-Go Quiches

These quiches are great to make on Sundays to enjoy all week. They keep well in the fridge and can be reheated at work or school!

Nutrition

340 calories per serving | Makes 4 servings

24 grams of fat

20 grams of protein

5 grams of net carbs

Ingredients

- 4 oz. roma tomato
- 2 oz. red onion
- 6 oz. white or brown mushrooms
- 12 large eggs
- ½ cup heavy cream

Instructions

1. Dice the roma tomato, red onion and mushrooms and cook them on medium heat until the onion is translucent, about 8 minutes.
2. Meanwhile, whisk together the eggs and heavy cream in a large bowl until very pale.
3. Add the cooked veggies to the bowl and stir.
4. Add the batter evenly into a lightly greased muffin tin and bake at 350°F for 25 minutes.
5. Let cool completely before removing. Store in an airtight container in the refrigerator and warm them up before enjoying. They may be frozen to enjoy later!

Cauliflower Hash Browns

What can't cauliflower do? It's a magical vegetable that can take the form of many of your favorite foods. Hash browns are no exception!

Nutrition

116 calories per serving | Makes 2 servings

- 8.5 grams of fat
- 5.5 grams of protein
- 4 grams of net carbs

Ingredients

- 150 grams cauliflower
- 1 large egg
- 1 stalk green onion
- ½ tsp. garlic powder
- ¼ cup sour cream

Instructions

1. Rice the cauliflower using a cheese grater into small pieces. Combine with the egg, chopped green onion and garlic powder in a mixing bowl.
2. With your hands, form flat patties about 4 inches in diameter.
3. In a well greased pan on low-medium heat, fry until golden brown on both sides. This should take about 5–8 minutes per side.
4. Enjoy with a dollop of sour cream.

High Fiber, High Crunch Cereal

Missing your bowl of cereal in the mornings? Make your own that's high in fat, fiber and protein to keep you full and energized!

Nutrition

350 calories per serving | Makes 2 servings

| 30 grams of fat
| 11 grams of protein
| 5 grams of net carbs

Ingredients

- ½ cup unsweetened coconut flakes
- 2 oz. almonds, whole or chopped
- 2 tbsp. chia seeds
- 2 cups unsweetened almond milk
- 10 drops liquid stevia (optional)

Instructions

1. Start by toasting the coconut flakes in the oven at 350°F for 5 minutes, stirring or rotating occasionally to avoid burning.
2. Combine almonds, chia seeds and the toasted coconut flakes in 2 serving bowls.
3. Pour the almond milk over both and sweeten with stevia if desired.
4. Stir and enjoy!

Goat Cheese Frittata

Frittatas are great for a large family breakfast or even for dinner. And if you've got leftover veggies, this is the recipe to make to use them all up!

Nutrition

410 calories per serving | Makes 4 servings

- 32 grams of fat
- 26 grams of protein
- 4 grams of net carbs

🕐 **Prep Time: 15 mins | Cook Time: 15 mins**

Ingredients

- 16 spears asparagus
- 4 oz. white or brown mushrooms
- 12 large eggs
- ½ cup heavy cream
- 4 oz. goat cheese or feta cheese

Instructions

1. Cut the fibrous ends off the asparagus and slice the mushrooms. Cook them in a well-oiled 10" cast iron skillet until slightly browned and softened.
2. Whisk the eggs and heavy cream until very pale. Season with salt and pepper.
3. Add the beaten eggs into the cast iron skillet and crumble the goat cheese or feta cheese on top.
4. Bake at 375°F for 15 minutes, let cool lightly and enjoy.

Breakfast Burritos

You don't have to go out for burritos — you can make them at home with some creamy scrambled eggs and spicy jalapeños!

Nutrition

320 calories per serving | Makes 2 servings

25 grams of fat	
18 grams of protein	
2 grams of net carbs	

🕐 **Prep Time: 5 mins | Cook Time: 5 mins**

Ingredients

- 2 tbsp. butter or coconut oil
- 6 large eggs
- 1 roma tomato, diced
- Sliced pickled jalapeños, to taste
- 2 large butter lettuce leaves

Instructions

1. Melt the butter and scramble the eggs in it on medium heat until they're just almost cooked throughout. Take the pan off the heat to let the eggs finish cooking.
2. Add tomato and jalapeño slices to the butter lettuce leaves. Then add the scrambled eggs and season with salt and pepper.
3. Roll up the butter lettuce leaves and enjoy now or pack away for later!

Peanut & Cacao Nib Pudding

Make-ahead recipes just got easier. With only 5 ingredients, this chia seed pudding is full of flavor, fiber and will save you precious minutes!

Nutrition

280 calories per serving | Makes 2 servings

| 20 grams of fat
| 9 grams of protein
| 5 grams of net carbs

🕐 **Prep Time: 5 mins | Passive Time: 12 hrs**

Ingredients

- 1 ½ cups unsweetened almond milk
- 2 tbsp. chia seeds
- 2 tbsp. peanut butter (or almond butter)
- 10 drops liquid stevia
- 30 grams cacao nibs (or SF chocolate chips)

Instructions

1. The night before, combine the almond milk, chia seeds, peanut butter (or almond butter) and liquid stevia in a mixing bowl and whisk until the nut butter is well incorporated.
2. Transfer to a serving dish and cover with plastic wrap. Refrigerate overnight.
3. In the morning, top with cacao nibs (or sugar-free chocolate chips) and enjoy!

French Brie Soufflé

Fancy doesn't always mean difficult. Take our French brie soufflé, for example. Only 5 ingredients means you can dine like a king in no time!

Nutrition

525 calories per serving | Makes 2 servings

- 47 grams of fat
- 22 grams of protein
- 2 grams of net carbs

Ingredients

- ¼ cup unsalted butter, melted
- ¼ cup almond flour
- 4 large eggs, separated
- 2 oz. brie cheese, cubed
- ½ cup unsweetened almond milk

Instructions

1. Combine the butter and almond flour in a pan over low heat. Stir until thickened.
2. Whisk the egg yolks into the mixture as well as the brie and a pinch of salt. Stir well.
3. Add almond milk slowly, stirring until combined.
4. Beat the egg whites with a pinch of salt until stiff peaks form. Then, fold them very gently into the entire mixture.
5. Pour the batter into 4 well-greased ramekins, broil for 3 minutes then bake for 20 minutes at 400°F.

Powerhouse Shake

If you're constantly running out the door, make yourself a breakfast in a bottle by combining caffeine, fat & protein!

Nutrition

425 calories per serving | Makes 2 servings

- 38 grams of fat
- 26 grams of protein
- 1 gram of net carbs

⏱ **Prep Time: 8 mins | Cook Time: 0 mins**

Ingredients

- 2 espresso shots
- 62 grams low-carb protein powder (see p. 22)
- ½ cup heavy cream
- 2 tbsp. coconut oil
- ½ tsp. ground cinnamon

Instructions

1. Pour the brewed espresso shots into a blender along with the protein powder (flavor of your choice), heavy cream, coconut oil and cinnamon.
2. Add about a cup of ice cubes, sweeten if desired, and blend on high until creamy and frothy.
3. Pour into a couple of mason jars with some more ice to take breakfast with you on-the-go.

Spinach & Feta Scramble

Feta really gives scrambled eggs a great flavor and texture. The spinach gives you a boost of vitamins right when you wake up!

Nutrition

465 calories per serving | Makes 2 servings

- 36 grams of fat
- 29 grams of protein
- 2 grams of net carbs

🕒 **Prep Time: 5 mins | Cook Time: 15 mins**

Ingredients

- 2 tbsp. unsalted butter
- 2 cups fresh spinach
- 4 strips bacon
- 6 large eggs
- 2 oz. feta cheese

Instructions

1. Melt the butter in a pan and cook the spinach until wilted. In another pan, cook the bacon strips until desired crispiness.
2. Whisk the eggs in a small bowl and add them to the hot pan with the spinach.
3. Stir continuously until almost fully cooked, then crumble the feta into the pan.
4. Season with salt and pepper and remove from the heat to continue cooking all the way.
5. Serve with the bacon strips and enjoy!

Sweet Raspberry Porridge

This sweet raspberry porridge is the perfect recipe for cold winter mornings. It can even be ready before your coffee finishes brewing!

Nutrition

333 calories per serving | Makes 2 servings

- 32 grams of fat
- 6 grams of protein
- 5 grams of net carbs

Ingredients

- 2 cups unsweetened almond milk
- ¼ cup flaxseed meal
- ¼ cup coconut flour
- 60 grams raspberries
- 10 drops liquid stevia (optional)

Instructions

1. Heat the almond milk in a pan or small pot.
2. Once it's steamy, add in flaxseed meal and coconut flour. Stir until combined.
3. Add in the raspberries and cook until the whole mixture thickens and the raspberries stain the porridge.
4. Sweeten with stevia if desired and enjoy!

Cheesy Breakfast Pizza

Feeling like pizza? Don't let the time stop you! Make a quick, low-carb breakfast pizza and have yourself a hearty meal.

Nutrition

400 calories per serving | Makes 2 servings

32 grams of fat	
26 grams of protein	
4 grams of net carbs	

🕐 **Prep Time: 5 mins | Cook Time: 10 mins**

Ingredients

- 1 cup shredded mozzarella (see p. 22)
- ½ cup marinara sauce
- 2 large eggs, fried
- 2 oz. pepperoni, sliced
- 6 leaves fresh basil

Instructions

1. Spread the shredded mozzarella cheese onto a small frying pan on medium heat and let it melt, slightly browning on the bottom.
2. Add marinara sauce and the fried eggs. Top with pepperoni slices and cook covered for about 3 minutes.
3. Wedge a spatula under the cheese and gently remove the pizza. Top with fresh basil.

Low-Carb Granola

Granola is the perfect addition to your favorite breakfast. Enjoy this over a few spoonfuls of yogurt, a smoothie or as a bowl of cereal!

Nutrition

275 calories per serving | Makes 4 servings

| 25 grams of fat
| 10 grams of protein
| 3 grams of net carbs

Ingredients

- 1 cup whole almonds
- ¼ cup sunflower seeds
- ¼ cup pumpkin seeds
- 1 tbsp. coconut oil
- 15 drops liquid stevia

Instructions

1. Add the almonds, sunflower seeds and pumpkin seeds to a food processor and pulse a few times until they're roughly chopped.
2. Add coconut oil, stevia and a pinch of salt. Pulse again to coat evenly.
3. Spread the mixture onto a baking sheet in a thin layer and bake at 350°F for about 10 minutes or until golden brown.
4. Let cool and store in an airtight jar.

Tip: *Enjoy by itself like a cereal with unsweetened almond milk or crumble onto yogurt and smoothies!*

Choco-Peanut Butter Shake

Who can resist the heavenly combo of chocolate and peanut butter? Who's opposed to having it for breakfast? No one, that's who.

Nutrition

450 calories per serving | Makes 2 servings

■ 33 grams of fat

■ 33 grams of protein

■ 4.5 grams of net carbs

🕐 **Prep Time: 5 mins | Cook Time: 0 mins**

Ingredients

- 2 cups unsweetened almond milk
- 62 grams low-carb chocolate protein powder (see p. 22)
- ¼ cup peanut butter
- 2 tbsp. coconut oil
- 10 ice cubes

Instructions

1. Combine all the ingredients in a blender.
2. Blend on high until everything is well combined.
3. Enjoy!

Tip: *If you don't have chocolate flavored protein powder, use vanilla or unflavored protein powder and add 1–2 tablespoons of unsweetened cocoa powder.*

Mediterranean Shakshuka

Poaching your eggs in marinara sauce makes a great, flavorful breakfast that's unusual, yet warm and inviting. Try it with feta and olives!

Nutrition

300 calories per serving | Makes 2 servings

- 22 grams of fat
- 18 grams of protein
- 5 grams of net carbs

Ingredients

- 1 cup marinara sauce
- 4 large eggs
- 2 oz. feta cheese
- 10 olives, chopped
- Fresh parsley

Instructions

1. Heat up the marinara sauce in a small skillet on high heat. Once the marinara is hot, crack the eggs in, spaced evenly apart.
2. Crumble the feta and chopped olives over the top of the eggs.
3. Bake at 400°F for about 10 minutes or until the eggs are slightly set on top.
4. Sprinkle with fresh parsley, let cool lightly and enjoy!

Buttery Flaxseed Muffins

Flaxseeds give a great texture and add a ton of fiber to foods. They retain their natural moisture to make super juicy muffins!

Nutrition

205 calories per serving | Makes 4 servings

18 grams of fat	
6 grams of protein	
3 grams of net carbs	

Ingredients

- 1 cup flaxseed meal
- 6 tbsp. granular erythritol
- 1 tsp. baking powder
- 2 large eggs
- ¼ cup unsalted butter, melted

Instructions

1. Combine the flaxseed meal, erythritol and baking powder and whisk well.
2. Add in the eggs and melted butter. Stir until well combined.
3. Pour into a lightly greased muffin tin and bake at 350°F for about 12 minutes.
4. Enjoy with some more butter!

Poached Eggs & Greens

A salad-inspired breakfast can be a refreshing break from the cooked, fried and baked breakfasts you may be used to.

Nutrition

400 calories per serving | Makes 2 servings

- 32 grams of fat
- 22 grams of protein
- 3 grams of net carbs

⏱ **Prep Time: 10 mins | Cook Time: 15 mins**

Ingredients

- 4 large eggs
- 6 strips bacon
- ¼ red onion, sliced
- 2 handfuls baby spinach
- ¼ tsp. paprika

Instructions

1. Gently poach the eggs in lightly boiling water for about 3 minutes each.
2. Cook the bacon strips and the red onion together until crispy.
3. Chop the bacon strips and add them and the red onion onto a bed of fresh baby spinach.
4. Pour a tablespoon of bacon grease onto each salad as a dressing. Season with salt and pepper and toss well.
5. Add the poached eggs on top and a sprinkle of paprika. Enjoy!

Pepper Bacon Omelet

This open-faced pepper bacon omelet is quick to make and has tons of flavor. If you've never tried mayo in an omelet, here's your chance!

Nutrition

475 calories per serving | Makes 2 servings

- 36 grams of fat
- 32 grams of protein
- 3 grams of net carbs

🕐 **Prep Time: 5 mins | Cook Time: 15 mins**

Ingredients

- 4 strips bacon
- ½ red bell pepper, chopped
- 6 large eggs, beaten
- 2 tbsp. mayonnaise
- ¼ cup shredded mozzarella (see p. 22)

Instructions

1. Cook bacon on medium heat on one side until crispy.
2. Flip the bacon and add chopped bell pepper in to cook in the bacon grease.
3. After that has cooked, set it all aside on a plate and chop the bacon into bits.
4. Add the eggs into the hot bacon grease and let cook halfway, scrambling them slightly.
5. Add the bell pepper, bacon bits, mayonnaise (spread lightly around the omelet) and cover with shredded mozzarella on top. Cook covered for about 5 minutes.
6. Season with salt and pepper. Enjoy!

Lunch
IN FIVE

30 *low-carb* lunches

Up to **5** net carbs, **5** ingredients & **5** easy steps for every recipe

Savory French Crepe'wiches

We all know fruity, chocolatey crepes, but have you ever tried savory ones? You'll never look at crepes the same way again!

Nutrition

450 calories per serving | Makes 2 servings

- 34 grams of fat
- 32 grams of protein
- 2 grams of net carbs

Ingredients

- 2 large eggs
- 2 oz. cream cheese
- 4 oz. cheddar cheese, shredded or sliced
- 4 oz. deli ham, sliced
- 1 tbsp. Dijon mustard

Instructions

1. Whisk the eggs and cream cheese together until smooth.
2. Add ¼ of the batter onto a very hot, lightly oiled frying pan. Spread quickly and thinly to reach the edges of the pan. Cook for 2 minutes, flip and cook the other side for 2 minutes. Repeat 3 more times until all the batter is cooked.
3. Add 1 oz. of cheddar, 1 oz. of ham and 1 teaspoon of Dijon mustard per crepe. Fold crepes to enclose the fillings and fry on the folded side for 20 seconds to seal it all in.
4. Cut diagonally and serve 4 triangles per serving.

Asian Beef Slaw

Just because there's only 5 ingredients, doesn't mean this slaw is low on flavor. Juicy ground beef and tender veggies make a perfect combination.

Nutrition

480 calories per serving | Makes 4 servings

26 grams of fat

48 grams of protein

5 grams of net carbs

Ingredients

- 1 medium carrot
- 1 small green cabbage
- 1 lb. ground beef
- 2 tbsp. soy sauce
- 1 stalk green onion

Instructions

1. Shred the carrot and small cabbage.
2. Add the ground beef to a large frying pan or wok and break it up with a wooden spoon until very fine. Cook until browned.
3. Once browned, about 5–10 minutes, add in the shredded carrot, cabbage, soy sauce, and salt and pepper to taste. Toss well and cook for 5 minutes or until the cabbage has wilted.
4. Serve with chopped green onion and enjoy!

Coconut Chicken Curry

Coconut cream adds moisture and sweetness to this simple chicken curry. It makes for a great, high-fat lunch with some fresh green beans!

Nutrition

325 calories per serving | Makes 4 servings

- 16 grams of fat
- 38 grams of protein
- 5 grams of net carbs

🕐 **Prep Time: 10 mins | Cook Time: 40 mins**

Ingredients

- ½ white onion, diced
- 24 oz. boneless skinless chicken thighs
- 14 oz. unsweetened canned coconut milk
- 2 cups green beans
- 1 tbsp. curry powder

Instructions

1. In an oiled pan on medium heat, cook onions until translucent, then take them off the pan.
2. Turn the heat up to high and once the pan is very hot, sear the chicken thighs for 3–5 minutes on each side. Then shred them using two forks or meat-shredding claws.
3. Combine shredded chicken, onion, coconut milk, chopped green beans, curry powder, salt and pepper in the pan and simmer on low for 20 minutes. The chicken should be fully cooked through and the green beans tender. Enjoy!

Miracle Spaghetti Bolognese

Saucy *Miracle Noodles* make this a healthy, light lunch with tons of flavor. Tiny, meaty chunks make this dish all about the fun noodles.

Nutrition

345 calories per serving | Makes 2 servings

24 grams of fat

27 grams of protein

3.5 grams of net carbs

Ingredients

- 1 bag *Miracle Noodle* Spaghetti
- 1 lb. ground beef
- 2 cups marinara sauce
- 1 tsp. dried basil
- ½ cup shredded or shaved Parmesan cheese

Instructions

1. Prepare the *Miracle Noodle* Spaghetti according to the package instructions.
2. In a hot, oiled pan, brown the ground beef. Once it has almost fully cooked, add in the marinara sauce and simmer for 5 minutes.
3. Stir in the Miracle Spaghetti and season with salt, pepper and dried basil.
4. Serve topped with Parmesan.

Classic Deviled Eggs

Eggs are so versatile! Take your basic boiled egg and turn it into a culinary masterpiece with the addition of a few key ingredients.

Nutrition

400 calories per serving | Makes 4 servings

- 34 grams of fat
- 19 grams of protein
- 2 grams of net carbs

🕐 **Prep Time: 15 mins | Cook Time: 10 mins**

Ingredients

- 12 large eggs
- 1 shallot, finely diced
- 1 tbsp. Dijon mustard
- ½ cup mayonnaise
- 1 lime, juiced

Instructions

1. Set a pot of water to boil and lower your eggs in gently using a spoon. Let them boil for 10 minutes.
2. Peel and halve the boiled eggs, scooping the yolks out into a large mixing bowl. Set aside the whites.
3. Add in the shallots, mustard, mayonnaise, lime juice, salt and pepper into the egg yolks. Mash until smooth.
4. Spoon the egg yolk mixture back into the egg whites and serve chilled.

Tip: *Use a piping bag to pipe out the egg yolks for a more beautiful presentation!*

Jalapeño Chicken Casserole

A little spice and a whole lot of flavor will keep your friends and family coming back for more with this delicious jalapeño chicken casserole.

Nutrition

610 calories per serving | Makes 4 servings

- 47 grams of fat
- 44 grams of protein
- 5 grams of net carbs

Ingredients

- 1 lb. boneless skinless chicken thighs
- 3 cups broccoli florets
- ½ cup mayonnaise
- 2 ½ cups cheddar cheese, grated
- 1 fresh jalapeño, sliced

Instructions

1. Fry the chicken thighs in a well-oiled pan on medium heat until cooked. Shred them with 2 forks or meat-shredding claws.
2. Chop the broccoli florets and combine them with the chicken, mayonnaise, 2 cups of cheddar, and salt and pepper in a 9×13" casserole dish. Bake for 25 minutes at 350°F.
3. In last 5 minutes of baking, top with the remaining cheddar and jalapeño slices.

Cauliflower Stir-Fried Rice

Everyone loves Chinese food leftovers but not the carbs and calories! Cauliflower rice is here to make things low-carb and even more delicious.

Nutrition

420 calories per serving | Makes 2 servings

- 20 grams of fat
- 52 grams of protein
- 5 grams of net carbs

Ingredients

- 1 lb. boneless skinless chicken thighs, cubed
- 300 grams cauliflower florets
- 2 tbsp. unsalted butter
- 50 grams carrot, grated
- 50 grams broccoli, diced

Instructions

1. Add the cubed chicken to an oiled wok or deep skillet and fry on medium-high heat for 5 minutes or until almost fully cooked.
2. Meanwhile, pulse the cauliflower florets in a food processor until they resemble rice.
3. Add the riced cauliflower, butter, carrot and broccoli to the wok and fry for an additional 5–8 minutes, stirring continuously.
4. Season generously with salt and pepper and serve.

Cheesy Tuna Melt

Quick and tasty, our tuna melt is a favorite and an important staple in a keto diet. Nothing beats the speed and simplicity of this recipe.

Nutrition

482 calories per serving | Makes 2 servings

- 37 grams of fat
- 31 grams of protein
- 4 grams of net carbs

🕐 **Prep Time: 10 mins | Cook Time: 10 mins**

Ingredients

- ½ medium red onion, diced
- 8 oz. canned tuna
- 4 tbsp. mayonnaise
- 2 large eggs
- 2 oz. mozzarella cheese, shredded

Instructions

1. Cook the red onion in a well-oiled pan on medium heat for 5 minutes or until softened.
2. Drain the canned tuna and add it along with the rest of the ingredients to the pan. Salt and pepper everything to taste.
3. Stir the mixture together until the egg has cooked and the mozzarella has melted, about 2 minutes, and serve.

Roasted Tomato Soup

This creamy roasted tomato soup is naturally sweet and super velvety. It's perfect for cold winter mornings or even chilled on hot summer days!

Nutrition

330 calories per serving | Makes 4 servings

- 25 grams of fat
- 2 grams of protein
- 5 grams of net carbs

Ingredients

- 14 oz. plum tomatoes, halved
- 100 grams yellow onion, diced
- 4 tbsp. unsalted butter
- 1 cup heavy cream
- 1 bunch fresh basil

Instructions

1. Broil the tomatoes face down on a baking sheet in the oven until the skin is blistered, about 5–10 minutes. Rotate the pan occasionally to prevent burning. Let them cool slightly and peel and discard the skins.
2. In a lightly oiled soup pot on medium heat, cook the diced onion until translucent.
3. Add butter, cream, 2 cups of water and the roasted tomatoes. Season generously with salt and pepper.
4. Let the soup simmer for 20 minutes, adding the bunch of basil in the last 5 minutes.
5. Transfer everything to a blender and blend on high until smooth. Enjoy!

Poached Egg & Roasted Veg

Poached eggs are a favorite for brunch. Try this delicious, dairy-free option for lunch for a boost of healthy veggies and fats.

Nutrition

345 calories per serving | Makes 2 servings

- 25 grams of fat
- 20 grams of protein
- 5 grams of net carbs

Ingredients

- 6 oz. white or brown mushrooms
- 10 spears asparagus
- 4 oz. breakfast sausage
- 1 roma tomato, chopped or sliced
- 2 large eggs, poached

Instructions

1. Chop the mushrooms and arrange them on a baking sheet with the asparagus. Drizzle with oil and broil for 4–6 minutes or until browned slightly.
2. Remove the sausage meat from its casing and cook it in a hot, oiled pan, breaking it up with a wooden spoon.
3. Combine the roasted veggies and fresh tomato on a plate and season with salt and pepper.
4. Add the cooked breakfast sausage and top with a poached egg. Enjoy!

Traditional Egg Salad

It couldn't be simpler to make this creamy, tangy egg salad! Make a big batch and enjoy this tasty, low-carb lunch all week long.

Nutrition

350 calories per serving | Makes 2 servings

| 29 grams of fat
| 19 grams of protein
| 1 gram of net carbs

Ingredients

- 6 large eggs, boiled
- 3 tbsp. mayonnaise
- 2 tsp. fresh parsley, chopped
- 1 tsp. paprika
- 2 tsp. lemon juice

Instructions

1. Chop the boiled eggs and add them to a mixing bowl along with the rest of the ingredients.
2. Season everything with salt and pepper to taste and mix very well. The mixture should be more creamy than chunky, but it can vary based on preference.
3. Serve chilled and enjoy!

Bacon Cauliflower Chowder

The tasty flavor of bacon completes any soup! Try fried, crispy strips on a creamy cauliflower chowder for a light lunch.

Nutrition

275 calories per serving | Makes 4 servings

- 19 grams of fat
- 15 grams of protein
- 5 grams of net carbs

🕐 **Prep Time: 15 mins | Cook Time: 60 mins**

Ingredients

- 1 large cauliflower
- 1 white onion, diced
- 1 small carrot, shredded
- ½ cup sour cream
- 16 slices bacon

Instructions

1. Chop cauliflower and add the florets to an oiled soup pot with the onion and carrot. Season very well and cook until the onion is translucent and other vegetables are soft.
2. Add 4 cups of water and bring to a boil. Lower to a simmer for 1 hour, stirring occasionally.
3. In the last few minutes, mix in the sour cream.
4. Fry the bacon strips until crispy, chop them up and add to each soup bowl when serving.

Chicken Avocado Salad

Grilled chicken and fresh avocado is lifted with the simple addition of lime juice! You'll swear this was a gourmet recipe!

Nutrition

300 calories per serving | Makes 2 servings

16 grams of fat

32 grams of protein

4 grams of net carbs

Ingredients

- 8 oz. boneless skinless chicken thighs
- 1 medium avocado
- 2 roma tomatoes
- 1 handful lettuce
- 1 lime, juiced

Instructions

1. Grill or fry the chicken thighs until fully cooked, about 5–8 minutes on each side.
2. Cube or slice the avocado and roma tomatoes. Shred the lettuce into bite-sized pieces.
3. Shred the chicken thighs using two forks or meat-shredding claws and combine everything in a large salad bowl.
4. Season with salt and pepper to taste and add the juice of a whole lime. Toss and enjoy!

Juicy Tuna Salad

You can't beat the classics! We love this tuna salad recipe because it's juicy, packed with protein and fills you up fast!

Nutrition

375 calories per serving | Makes 2 servings

- 22 grams of fat
- 39 grams of protein
- 4 grams of net carbs

⏱ **Prep Time: 10 mins | Cook Time: 0 mins**

Ingredients

- 2 stalks celery
- ½ medium red onion
- 2 large eggs, boiled
- 12 oz. canned tuna
- 3 tbsp. mayonnaise

Instructions

1. Thinly chop the celery and dice the onion and eggs.
2. Drain the canned tuna and add all the ingredients into a bowl.
3. Salt and pepper to taste and mix everything well.
4. Serve and enjoy!

Coconut Macadamia Shake

Coconut cashew is one of the best flavor combos, but macadamias are much lower in carbs and higher in fat! So throw 'em in your lunch shake!

Nutrition

390 calories per serving | Makes 1 serving

38 grams of fat

3 grams of protein

4 grams of net carbs

Ingredients

- 2 cups unsweetened almond milk
- 1 oz. macadamia nuts
- ¼ cup unsweetened coconut flakes
- ½ tsp. ground cinnamon
- 10 drops liquid stevia

Instructions

1. Combine all the ingredients in a blender or Nutribullet and blend on high until very creamy, about 1–2 minutes.
2. Sweeten with stevia to taste. You can substitute with erythritol if you don't like the taste of stevia.
3. Serve cold and enjoy!

Cheddar Chips & Guacamole

This popular appetizer turned low-carb is surprisingly filling! Lots of healthy fats from avocado and cheddar cheese make this a delicious lunch.

Nutrition

420 calories per serving | Makes 1 serving

- 35 grams of fat
- 16 grams of protein
- 5 grams of net carbs

Ingredients

- 2 oz. cheddar cheese, shredded
- 1 avocado
- ½ roma tomato, diced
- 1 tbsp. white onion, diced
- 1 tbsp. lime juice

Instructions

1. Add the shredded cheddar in a thin layer to a pan on medium heat. Let it melt and caramelize until golden all around, about 10 minutes. When it has solidified and browned a bit, flip it and cook for another 2 minutes.
2. Mash together the avocado, tomato, onion and lime juice. Season with salt and pepper.
3. Serve together and enjoy!

Chicken Salad-Stuffed Avocado

Avocado shells are a great alternative to boring bowls! We love adding in creamy chicken salad and being the envy of our friends.

Nutrition

570 calories per serving | Makes 1 serving

| 45 grams of fat
| 29 grams of protein
| 5 grams of net carbs

🕐 **Prep Time: 10 mins | Cook Time: 10 mins**

Ingredients

- 3 oz. chicken breast
- 1 tbsp. red onion, diced
- 1 celery stalk, diced
- 1 medium avocado
- ⅓ cup sour cream

Instructions

1. Cook the chicken on low heat until fully cooked. Then shred it using two forks.
2. Combine chicken, onion and celery in a bowl.
3. Cut and pit an avocado. Scoop some of the avocado out and add it to the bowl.
4. Add in the sour cream, salt and pepper to the bowl and toss everything well.
5. Scoop the chicken salad mix back into the avocado halves and enjoy!

Cashew Chicken Stir-Fry

Here's a lighter lunch option that you can always add to! Asian veggies and *Miracle Rice* makes this a great alternative to unhealthy take-out.

Nutrition

285 calories per serving | Makes 4 servings

- 17 grams of fat
- 28 grams of protein
- 4.5 grams of net carbs

Ingredients

- 2 bags *Miracle Noodle* Rice
- 1 lb. boneless skinless chicken thighs, cubed
- 20 spears asparagus
- ½ cup whole cashews
- 2 tbsp. soy sauce

Instructions

1. Prepare the *Miracle Noodle Rice* according to the package instructions.
2. Cook the chicken thighs in a well-oiled pan on medium heat until almost fully cooked.
3. Cut the fibrous ends off the asparagus (about 2 inches). Add the asparagus, cashews and soy sauce into the pan.
4. Let simmer, stirring, for 8 minutes.
5. Add *Miracle Rice*, stir for 2 minutes and serve.

Chicken-Wrapped Bacon Bites

Finger foods make eating fun! Be the envy of your coworkers when you whip these out of your lunchbox at break time!

Nutrition

575 calories per serving | Makes 2 servings

44 grams of fat

44 grams of protein

2 grams of net carbs

🕐 **Prep Time: 15 mins | Cook Time: 10 mins**

Ingredients

- 6 strips bacon
- 4 oz. chicken breast
- 2 stalks green onion
- 2 tbsp. mayonnaise
- 1 tsp. hot sauce of choice

Instructions

1. Cut the bacon in half to make 12 strips.
2. Cube the chicken into 12 bite-sized pieces and chop the green onion into 2" pieces.
3. Place a chicken cube and green onion piece onto the end of one bacon strip and roll the bacon tightly wrapping the contents.
4. Cook on a lightly oiled pan on medium heat for about 10 minutes, flipping occasionally.
5. Serve with mayonnaise mixed with hot sauce.

Lemon Kale Salad

You can keep this lemon kale salad vegetarian, or add your favorite protein to it. It's fresh, tangy and so easy to make.

Nutrition

420 calories per serving | Makes 2 servings

41 grams of fat

9 grams of protein

5 grams of net carbs

🕐 **Prep Time: 10 mins | Cook Time: 0 mins**

Ingredients

- 4 oz. fresh kale
- 2 oz. feta cheese
- 30 grams slivered almonds
- 1 lemon, juiced
- ¼ cup olive oil

Instructions

1. Rinse and rip the kale leaves and add them to a salad bowl with the lemon juice and olive oil. Massage for a few minutes to soften the leaves.
2. Crumble the feta into the bowl and add the slivered almonds.
3. Season with a bit of salt, toss well and enjoy!

Tip: *Massaging the kale leaves with lemon juice and olive oil will help them soften and become less bitter.*

129

Cheeseburger Crepes

You'll wonder why you didn't think of this sooner — cheeseburger stuffed savory crepes! Super low-carb and super portable!

Nutrition

520 calories per serving | Makes 2 servings

- 36 grams of fat
- 38 grams of protein
- 3.5 grams of net carbs

Ingredients

- ½ yellow onion, diced
- ½ lb. ground beef
- 2 oz. cheddar cheese
- 2 large eggs
- 2 oz. cream cheese

Instructions

1. Fry the onion and ground beef in an oiled pan on medium heat for 5 minutes. Add cheddar and mix well until melted.
2. Whisk the eggs and cream cheese together in a bowl until smooth. Add ¼ of the batter to a very hot, oiled pan. Tilt to coat the pan evenly and fry for 2 minutes. Flip and fry for 2 another minutes. Repeat for the rest of the batter.
3. Add the beef cheeseburger mix to the crepes and roll them up.
4. Slice in half and serve 2 full crepes (4 halves) per serving.

Pizza Casserole

This delicious pizza casserole includes the best part of any pizza but without the crust and a few extra tasty ingredients!

Nutrition

500 calories per serving | Makes 4 servings

- 34 grams of fat
- 42 grams of protein
- 5 grams of net carbs

🕐 **Prep Time: 15 mins | Cook Time: 35 mins**

Ingredients

- 1 lb. boneless skinless chicken thighs
- 12 oz. ricotta cheese
- 2 large zucchini, cubed
- 4 oz. pepperoni, sliced
- 1 cup shredded mozzarella (see p. 22)

Instructions

1. Fry the chicken thighs in an oiled pan on medium heat until cooked. Shred with 2 forks or meat-shredding claws.
2. Combine the ricotta, chicken, zucchini, half of the pepperoni slices, salt and pepper in a 9×13″ casserole dish and bake for 25 minutes at 350°F.
3. In last 5 minutes of baking, top with shredded mozzarella and the rest of the pepperoni slices. Finish baking and serve!

Taco Salad Bowl

You'll forget all about taco shells when you dig in to this taco salad bowl. It's got all the yummy flavors of a taco without all the carbs!

Nutrition

465 calories per serving | Makes 2 servings

- 33 grams of fat
- 31 grams of protein
- 4 grams of net carbs

Ingredients

- ½ lb. ground beef
- 1 small avocado
- 2 roma tomatoes
- 1 handful lettuce
- ½ cup shredded cheddar

Instructions

1. Brown the ground beef in a hot, oiled pan.
2. While it's cooking, cube the avocado and roma tomatoes.
3. Shred the lettuce into a salad bowl and add the avocado and roma tomatoes.
4. Throw in the ground beef and cheddar. Salt and pepper to taste.
5. Mix to combine everything and serve.

Tip: *For a quick dressing, just use a dollop of sour cream!*

Meatball Marinara Bake

Who needs spaghetti when you can make delicious, moist meatballs and enjoy them with loads of cheese? Best of all, you only need one pan!

Nutrition

420 calories per serving | Makes 8 servings

- 29 grams of fat
- 38 grams of protein
- 3 grams of net carbs

Ingredients

- 1 ½ lbs. ground beef
- 4 large eggs
- 1 cup grated Parmesan cheese
- 2 cups marinara sauce
- 2 cups shredded mozzarella

Instructions

1. Combine the beef, eggs, Parmesan and ½ teaspoon of salt. Make 1–1.5" inch meatballs.
2. In an oiled pan on high heat, sear the meatballs on all sides for about 3–5 minutes until they're browned.
3. Into a 9×9" casserole dish, add the marinara sauce and meatballs and bake for 20 minutes at 350°F.
4. Add mozzarella, broil for 2 minutes and serve.

Creamy Shrimp Curry

Shrimp often goes unnoticed in a sea of meat-laden dishes, but their texture really stands out in our delicate, creamy curry.

Nutrition

329 calories per serving | Makes 2 servings

- 18 grams of fat
- 49 grams of protein
- 5 grams of net carbs

Ingredients

- 1 large zucchini, diced
- 12 oz. large shrimp, peeled
- 2 tbsp. shelled edamame
- 1 tbsp. soy sauce
- 4 oz. cream cheese

Instructions

1. In an oiled pan on medium heat, fry the diced zucchini for about 7 minutes, stirring often.
2. Add the shrimp and let cook until fully pink.
3. Add in edamame, soy sauce and cream cheese to the pan and stir well for an additional 2 minutes or until the cream cheese has melted.
4. Salt and pepper to taste, serve and enjoy!

Loaded Cobb Salad

Cobb salads are a safe, low-carb option in restaurants, but who needs a restaurant to enjoy it? Make your own super filling lunch and enjoy!

Nutrition

400 calories per serving | Makes 2 servings

- 36 grams of fat
- 13 grams of protein
- 3 grams of net carbs

Ingredients

- 4 strips bacon, chopped
- 2 handfuls baby spinach
- 2 large eggs, hard boiled
- 1 small avocado
- 3 tbsp. ranch dressing

Instructions

1. Fry the chopped bacon in a pan on medium heat until you have crispy bite-sized pieces.
2. In the meantime, make a bed of baby spinach in two bowls.
3. Chop the eggs and avocado and divide them evenly into each bowl on top of the bed of baby spinach.
4. Add the fried bacon bits to each salad.
5. Top each salad with ranch dressing and serve!

Creamy Peppercorn Beef

Juicy beef only gets juicier with the addition of cream and the sweetness of onion. Try it on a bed of lettuce for some added crunch!

Nutrition

630 calories per serving | Makes 2 servings

- 50 grams of fat
- 46 grams of protein
- 4.5 grams of net carbs

🕐 **Prep Time: 10 mins | Cook Time: 30 mins**

Ingredients

- ½ white onion, sliced
- 1 lb. sirloin steak
- ¾ cup heavy cream
- 2 tbsp. peppercorns
- 2 handfuls romaine lettuce

Instructions

1. In an oiled pan on medium heat, cook onions until translucent, then take them off the pan.
2. Turn the heat up to high and when the pan is very hot, sear the sirloin steak for 5 minutes on each side. Then, slice the steak into strips.
3. Place onion and steak strips back into the pan with the cream and peppercorns. Salt to taste. Simmer for 5–10 mins and serve over a bed of romaine lettuce.

Bacon Turkey Wraps

Nothing beats some refreshing lettuce wraps. Forgo the processed, low-carb wraps in favor of something all natural!

Nutrition

585 calories per serving | Makes 1 serving

- 44 grams of fat
- 43 grams of protein
- 2 grams of net carbs

Ingredients

- 3 strips bacon
- 3 tsp. mayonnaise
- 3 lettuce leaves
- 3 oz. provolone cheese
- 3 oz. sliced turkey

Instructions

1. Cook bacon until crispy, then chop it into bits.
2. Add a teaspoon of mayonnaise to each lettuce leaf and then top each with a slice of provolone cheese.
3. Lay a slice of turkey onto each wrap and then sprinkle with the cooked bacon.
4. Roll each up tightly and enjoy or pack away!

Creamy Mushroom Soup

Delicate and creamy — this soup is quick to make and tastes like it's straight out of a restaurant! You'd never guess it's only got 5 ingredients.

Nutrition

320 calories per serving | Makes 4 servings

23 grams of fat

28 grams of protein

5 grams of net carbs

Ingredients

- 4 cups chicken broth
- ½ medium yellow onion, diced
- 12 oz. white or brown mushrooms, chopped
- 1 lb. boneless skinless chicken thighs
- ¾ cup heavy cream

Instructions

1. Add chicken broth, onion and mushrooms to a soup pot on medium heat.
2. Once at a boil, reduce heat to a simmer for 30 minutes. Salt and pepper to taste.
3. Fry chicken in an oiled pan on medium heat until cooked, about 6 minutes, then shred.
4. Add the chicken thighs and heavy cream to the pot and cook for an additional 10 minutes. Serve and enjoy!

Cabbage & Sausage Skillet

You'd never think two things like sausage and cabbage could go together so perfectly! Wilted cabbage is very reminiscent of noodles.

Nutrition

310 calories per serving | Makes 4 servings

| 25 grams of fat
| 13 grams of protein
| 5 grams of net carbs

Ingredients

- 4 Italian sausage links
- ½ head green cabbage, shredded
- 2 tbsp. unsalted butter
- ¼ cup sour cream
- ¼ cup mayonnaise

Instructions

1. Fully cook the sausage links in a pan and then slice them into bite-sized pieces.
2. In the same pan, wilt the cabbage in the butter, stirring occasionally.
3. Add the sausages back into the pan and add the sour cream and mayonnaise.
4. Season with salt and pepper and let simmer for about 10 minutes, stirring occasionally.

Dinner
IN FIVE

---

30 *low-carb* dinners

Up to **5** net carbs, **5** ingredients & **5** easy steps for every recipe

Soy Sauce Ginger Pork

Asian inspired, sweet & salty pork over some basic, but delicious green beans. Dinner couldn't be simpler!

Nutrition

335 calories per serving | Makes 2 servings

- 20 grams of fat
- 37 grams of protein
- 5 grams of net carbs

Ingredients

- 2 6-oz. pork loin chops
- 2 tbsp. sesame seed oil
- ¼ cup soy sauce
- 1 inch ginger, minced
- 1 cup green beans

Instructions

1. Heat up a pan with sesame seed oil. Cook ginger until fragrant, about 3–5 minutes.
2. Add pork loin to the pan and cook for about 8 minutes on each side. In the last 3 minutes, add soy sauce. Spoon the soy sauce to coat the pork well while cooking.
3. Cook green beans in another pan on high heat until slightly browned.
4. Slice the pork chops and serve over a bed of green beans. Add an extra drizzle of soy sauce for even more flavor!

Cheesy Meatballs Parm

Meatballs are a simple, low-carb dinner staple that are popular with kids and adults alike!

Nutrition

575 calories per serving | Makes 2 servings

| 35 grams of fat
| 52 grams of protein
| 4 grams of net carbs

🕐 **Prep Time: 10 mins | Cook Time: 15 mins**

Ingredients

- 1 lb. ground beef
- 1 large egg, beaten
- ¼ cup Parmesan cheese
- ½ cup marinara sauce
- 200 grams zucchini

Instructions

1. Combine beef, egg and Parmesan plus seasonings of your choice. Roll into 1" balls.
2. Pan sear meatballs on all sides on high heat. Lower flame, add marinara sauce and cook covered for 10 minutes.
3. Spiralize the zucchini into zoodles and cook them in a lightly oiled pan for no more than 2 minutes, tossing continuously.
4. Add meatballs to a bed of zoodles and enjoy!

Avocado Lime Salmon

One of our favorite salmon recipes is smothered in a zesty avocado lime sauce atop delicate riced cauliflower!

Nutrition

420 calories per serving | Makes 2 servings

27 grams of fat

37 grams of protein

5 grams of net carbs

Ingredients

- 2 6-oz. salmon fillets
- 1 medium avocado
- ½ lime, juiced
- 2 tbsp. red onion
- 100 grams cauliflower florets

Instructions

1. Rice the cauliflower florets in a food processor and cook them in an oiled pan on low heat, covered, for 8 minutes.
2. Blend the avocado, juice of ½ lime, salt & pepper until creamy and smooth. Set aside.
3. Heat a skillet on medium heat with some avocado or coconut oil and cook salmon for about 4–5 minutes on each side.
4. Serve with cauliflower rice and garnish with the avocado sauce and some diced red onion.

Lemon Rosemary Chicken

Grilled & seasoned simply, this flavorful chicken breast recipe is easy to make and pairs well with cauliflower mashed potatoes.

Nutrition

400 calories per serving | Makes 2 servings

26 grams of fat

39 grams of protein

3 grams of net carbs

Ingredients

- 2 8-oz. chicken breasts
- ½ lemon
- 1 sprig fresh rosemary
- ½ head cauliflower, broken into florets
- 4 tbsp. unsalted butter, melted

Instructions

1. Pound the chicken breasts until ½ inch thick.
2. Marinade them for an hour in the juice of ½ a lemon, salt, pepper and rosemary needles.
3. Steam the cauliflower florets, then blend them with butter. Season with salt and pepper.
4. Grill or fry the chicken breasts until cooked, about 7 minutes on each side.
5. Serve the chicken breast on a bed of the cauliflower mashed potatoes and enjoy!

Chicken Parmesan

An Italian classic turned low-carb with the help of one special ingredient! Make this recipe for dinner and enjoy juicy, crispy chicken breasts!

Nutrition

425 calories per serving | Makes 2 servings

| 23 grams of fat
| 52 grams of protein
| 2 grams of net carbs

⏱ **Prep Time: 10 mins | Cook Time: 30 mins**

Ingredients

- 2 6-oz. chicken breasts
- 1 large egg, beaten
- ¼ cup Parmesan cheese
- 2 oz. pork rinds
- ½ cup marinara sauce

Instructions

1. Pulse the pork rinds and Parmesan in a food processor until they resemble bread crumbs.
2. Coat the chicken breasts in the beaten egg then the low-carb breading, pressing firmly.
3. Bake the breaded chicken breasts in a 375°F oven for 30 minutes.
4. Add marinara sauce to each chicken breast 5 minutes before they're done cooking.
5. Serve with a sprinkle of more Parmesan cheese and dried spices of your choice (see page 27).

Sweet Pork Tenderloin

Craving something sweet? Some apple will do the trick — layered over pork tenderloin, it provides the perfect sweet pairing.

Nutrition

420 calories per serving | Makes 2 servings

28 grams of fat

37 grams of protein

5 grams of net carbs

Ingredients

- 2 6-oz. pork loin chops
- 40 grams sliced apple
- 2-4 sprigs rosemary
- 4 tbsp. unsalted butter
- 200 grams cauliflower

Instructions

1. Season pork loins with salt and pepper. Sear them on both sides in a well-oiled pan on high heat.
2. Lower the flame and add sliced apple and a sprig of rosemary to the top of the pork loins. Cover and cook for about 8 minutes.
3. Steam the cauliflower florets, then blend them with butter. Season with salt and pepper.
4. Serve the pork loin chops with a fresh sprig of rosemary and alongside the cauliflower mashed potatoes.

Sloppy Joe

A family favorite, now low-carb and under 5 ingredients! Enjoy it all on its own or on Oopsie rolls.

Nutrition

640 calories per serving | Makes 2 servings

| 50 grams of fat

■ 38 grams of protein

| 2 grams of net carbs

Ingredients

- 1 lb. ground beef
- ½ green bell pepper
- ½ cup marinara sauce
- 1 tbsp. Dijon mustard
- 1 tbsp. soy sauce

Instructions

1. Chop bell pepper and fry in an oiled pan on medium heat until softened.
2. Add the ground beef to the pan and break it up into small pieces using a wooden spoon.
3. Cook beef until brown, then add marinara, Dijon mustard and soy sauce. Season with salt and pepper to taste.
4. Continue to cook until the ground beef has cooked through and everything has thickened a bit.

Zesty Shrimp Skewers

Fun to make and more fun to eat! These zesty lemon skewers are full of flavor & pair nicely with our creamy avocado lime sauce.

Nutrition

440 calories per serving | Makes 2 servings

33 grams of fat

38 grams of protein

3 grams of net carbs

Ingredients

- 16 oz. large shrimp, peeled
- 1 medium avocado
- 3 tbsp. mayonnaise
- 1 lime
- 2 cups frisée (or baby spinach)

Instructions

1. Defrost shrimp if necessary and thread them onto bamboo skewers.
2. Fry or grill the shrimp for about 3 minutes on each side or until fully pink.
3. Blend the avocado, mayonnaise, the juice of one lime and salt and pepper together in a small blender.
4. Serve the shrimp on a bed of frisée (or baby spinach) and drizzle them with the zesty avocado lime sauce.

Tip: *Moisten the bamboo skewers before threading to prevent them from catching fire.*

Extra Crispy Chicken Thighs

There's nothing like a crisp skin on a juicy chicken thigh. In this recipe, you'll broil chicken thighs with lemon and garlic!

Nutrition

635 calories per serving | Makes 2 servings

- 46 grams of fat
- 43 grams of protein
- 3 grams of net carbs

Ingredients

- 4 boneless chicken thighs
- ½ lemon
- 2 cloves garlic, sliced thinly
- 4 tbsp. unsalted butter
- 200 grams zucchini

Instructions

1. Season the chicken thighs with lemon juice, salt and pepper.
2. Arrange sliced garlic on top and set them onto a baking sheet lined with a cooling rack. Bake at 350°F for 25 minutes.
3. Slice zucchini and fry in olive oil until softened.
4. Add a tablespoon of butter onto each thigh and broil for 5 minutes.
5. Enjoy the chicken thighs with fried zucchini.

168

Pork Chops in Mushroom Sauce

A delicate yet robust, creamy mushroom sauce drizzled over pork chops for a very filling dinner!

Nutrition

790 calories per serving | Makes 2 servings

| 53 grams of fat |
| 46 grams of protein |
| 5 grams of net carbs |

🕐 **Prep Time: 5 mins | Cook Time: 30 mins**

Ingredients

- ¼ white onion, diced
- 16 oz. white or brown mushrooms
- 2 tbsp. unsalted butter
- ½ cup heavy cream
- 2 8-oz. pork chops

Instructions

1. Start by sautéing the onion in an oiled pan until translucent.
2. Then add mushrooms and butter and cook until mushrooms have shrunk a bit. Add heavy cream and simmer sauce until it thickens, about 10 minutes.
3. In another pan, cook pork chops for 5–7 minutes on each side. Serve with the mushroom sauce.

171

Marinara Poached Cod

Delicate cod poached in a flavorful tomato sauce paired with green beans makes a great, light dinner!

Nutrition

390 calories per serving | Makes 2 servings

- 20 grams of fat
- 43 grams of protein
- 5 grams of net carbs

Ingredients

- 2 8-oz. cod fillets
- 2 tbsp. olive oil
- ½ cup marinara sauce
- 3 bay leaves
- 2 cups green beans

Instructions

1. Heat olive oil and marinara in a pan on medium heat. Add bay leaves, salt, pepper and a cup of water. Let it simmer for 5 minutes.
2. Lower the flame and add the cod fillets. Cover and cook for about 10 minutes, flipping once in between.
3. In another pan, sauté green beans in olive oil on medium-high heat for about 10 minutes.
4. Once the cod is cooked and opaque throughout, serve with the green beans and enjoy!

Buffalo Chicken Thighs

If you love buffalo wings, you'll love this recipe. These easy buffalo chicken thighs are a family favorite and are ultra low-carb.

Nutrition

745 calories per serving | Makes 2 servings

| 61 grams of fat
| 45 grams of protein
| 5 grams of net carbs

Ingredients

- 4 boneless chicken thighs
- ¼ cup *Frank's Red Hot sauce*
- 2 tbsp. unsalted butter
- 2 cups green beans
- ¼ cup Bleu cheese dressing

Instructions

1. In an oven-safe pan on high heat, sear the thighs skin side down until golden. Flip and transfer to the oven for 20 minutes at 375°F.
2. Melt the butter and *Frank's Red Hot* sauce together on a very low flame, whisking well.
3. Coat the cooked chicken thighs in Frank's.
4. Fry the green beans in an oiled pan on medium-high heat until slightly browned.
5. Serve everything with Bleu cheese dressing.

Cheese Shell Tacos

Ultra low-carb tacos in mere minutes! Fill them up with your favorite fillings — ours are creamy and spicy, feel free to adjust.

Nutrition

580 calories per 2 tacos | Makes 4 tacos

- 43 grams of fat
- 39 grams of protein
- 5 grams of net carbs

🕐 **Prep Time: 10 mins | Cook Time: 30 mins**

Ingredients

- 1 cup shredded mozzarella cheese
- ½ lb. ground beef
- ½ cup sour cream
- ½ cup guacamole
- Sliced jalapeños (optional)

Instructions

1. Set a pan onto medium heat and melt ¼ cup of mozzarella cheese at a time until brown and caramelized.

2. Wedge a spatula underneath and drape the shell across a wooden spoon on a pot or between two glasses to cool into a taco shape.

3. Cook the ground beef and season with salt, pepper and any spices of your choice (see page 27).

4. Divide the ground beef equally into each taco shell, plus 2 tablespoons of sour cream, 2 tablespoons of guacamole & jalapeño slices (optional).

Mustard Lemon Salmon

Delicate salmon seared and cooked in a mustard lemon sauce to make a tangy and creamy dinner!

Nutrition

465 calories per serving | Makes 2 servings

32 grams of fat

36 grams of protein

1 gram of net carbs

Ingredients

- 2 6-oz. salmon fillets
- ¼ cup heavy cream
- 1 tbsp. Dijon mustard
- 1 tbsp. lemon juice
- 100 grams cauliflower florets

Instructions

1. Rice the cauliflower in a food processor and cook in an oiled pan on low heat, covered, for 8 minutes, stirring ocassionally.
2. Heat another skillet on medium heat with olive oil and cook salmon for 3 minutes on each side. Then set aside.
3. Stir together heavy cream, mustard and lemon juice and add salmon back in for 5 minutes.
4. Serve everything on top of cauliflower rice.

Loaded Beef and Broccoli

Beef and broccoli makes dinner a breeze with common ingredients making it a go-to staple for your low-carb diet.

Nutrition

660 calories per serving | Makes 2 servings

- 41 grams of fat
- 60 grams of protein
- 5 grams of net carbs

Ingredients

- 100 grams broccoli
- 1 clove garlic
- 1 lb. ground beef
- 4 oz. shredded mozzarella
- 1 large egg

Instructions

1. Chop the broccoli and fry the florets in an oiled pan on high heat for 5–8 minutes.
2. Mince the garlic and add it in. Cook until fragrant and the broccoli softened.
3. Add the ground beef and break it up with a wooden spoon until cooked throughout.
4. Add the mozzarella cheese and the egg to mixture and stir well to incorporate.
5. Season with salt and pepper to taste and serve. Enjoy!

Soy Glazed Chicken

This Asian-inspired chicken marinade is absolutely delicious and will leave you craving more. Be sure to make plenty!

Nutrition

507 calories per serving | Makes 2 servings

▌ 38 grams of fat

▌ 38 grams of protein

▌ 3 grams of net carbs

🕐 **Prep Time: 35 mins | Cook Time: 20 mins**

Ingredients

- 4 boneless chicken thighs
- ¼ cup soy sauce
- 1 fresh jalapeño, minced
- 1 lemon
- 2 cups green beans

Instructions

1. Mix together the minced jalapeño, soy sauce, fresh lemon juice and chicken thighs in a large bowl. Marinate for at least 30 minutes.
2. Fry the marinated chicken thighs in a well-oiled pan on medium heat for 8–10 minutes on each side.
3. Cook green beans in another pan on medium-high heat until slightly browned, about 5–8 minutes.
4. Serve everything together and enjoy!

Lemon Garlic Salmon

Prep time for this dinner is a breeze! Just dress the salmon and steam it and serve on top of zucchini. Velvety soft fish in no time!

Nutrition

495 calories per serving | Makes 2 servings

36 grams of fat

35 grams of protein

3 grams of net carbs

Ingredients

- 2 6-oz. salmon fillets
- 2 cloves garlic
- 4 slices lemon
- 2 tbsp. olive oil
- 1 large zucchini

Instructions

1. On a baking sheet lined with 2 sheets of foil, add olive oil and place 1 salmon fillet onto each sheet of foil. Season with salt and pepper and top with 2 lemon slices each.
2. Slice the garlic and arrange around each salmon. Close each sheet of foil tightly and bake everything at 400°F for 15 minutes.
3. Spiralize the zucchini using a vegetable spiralizer and cook in a lightly oiled pan for no longer than 2 minutes, tossing continuously.
4. Serve the baked salmon on top of a bed of zoodles and enjoy!

Mediterranean Lamb Burger

Greek inspired & seasoned – this variation of a burger will leave you wanting seconds! Best served with creamed spinach.

Nutrition

640 calories per serving | Makes 2 servings

- 50 grams of fat
- 38 grams of protein
- 2 grams of net carbs

🕐 **Prep Time: 5 mins | Cook Time: 15 mins**

Ingredients

- 12 oz. ground lamb
- 1 tbsp. dried rosemary
- 2 oz. goat cheese
- 12 oz. spinach
- ¼ cup sour cream

Instructions

1. Season the lamb with salt, pepper and dried rosemary. Form two, flattened patties and grill or fry until cooked throughout.
2. Cook spinach in an oiled pan until wilted, then add sour cream. Mix well and season with salt and pepper.
3. Add an ounce of goat cheese onto each burger and serve with creamed spinach.

Chicken Zoodle Alfredo

A super creamy and simple dinner that's delightfully delicious! Break out the Parmesan cheese and enjoy liberally in this alfredo recipe!

Nutrition

521 calories per serving | Makes 2 servings

- 28 grams of fat
- 59 grams of protein
- 3 grams of net carbs

🕐 **Prep Time: 5 mins | Cook Time: 20 mins**

Ingredients

- 2 8-oz. chicken breasts
- ¼ cup heavy cream
- ¼ cup Parmesan cheese
- 2 tbsp. unsalted butter
- 200 grams zucchini

Instructions

1. Fry the chicken breasts for about 7 minutes on each side and then slice them into strips.
2. After the chicken is off the pan, lower the flame and melt the butter. Add in heavy cream, Parmesan and cook until thickened.
3. Spiralize the zucchini and pan fry for no longer than 2 minutes.
4. Add the chicken to the zoodles and drizzle with the alfredo sauce.

Baked Dijon Salmon

This is one of our favorite ways to prepare salmon! The Dijon gives it a unique flavor and the pork rind-Parmesan breading gives it a satisfying crunch.

Nutrition

415 calories per serving | Makes 2 servings

| 25 grams of fat
| 40 grams of protein
| 2 grams of net carbs

⏱ **Prep Time: 10 mins | Cook Time: 15 mins**

Ingredients

- 2 6-oz. salmon fillets
- 3 tbsp. Dijon mustard
- 1 oz. pork rinds
- 2 tbsp. Parmesan cheese
- 16 spears asparagus

Instructions

1. Rub the salmon fillets with Dijon mustard on all sides and season with salt and pepper.
2. Pulse the pork rinds and Parmesan cheese until they resemble bread crumbs.
3. Press the salmon firmly into the pork rind-Parmesan breading mixture on all sides.
4. Cut the fibrous ends off the asparagus.
5. Bake the salmon and asparagus on an oiled baking sheet at 400°F for 15 minutes. Enjoy!

Greek Lemon Chicken

Food of the gods! The quick prep and bake time makes dinner easy and delicious. Enjoy olives and spinach as traditional Greek sides.

Nutrition

634 calories per serving | Makes 2 servings

- 54 grams of fat
- 37 grams of protein
- 2 grams of net carbs

Ingredients

- 4 boneless chicken thighs
- ¼ cup olive oil
- 1 lemon
- 4 tbsp. olives
- 4 oz. spinach

Instructions

1. Squeeze the lemon juice into a bowl and add olive oil, salt, pepper and chicken thighs. Marinate for at least 30 minutes, but preferably 4 hours.
2. Bake the marinated chicken thighs at 375°F for 30 minutes.
3. Serve the thighs on a bed of spinach and olives. Add a squeeze of fresh lemon juice.

Creamy Shrimp Scampi

Creamy, saucy shrimp paired with even creamier cauliflower mash makes a great light dinner full of flavor.

Nutrition

660 calories per serving | Makes 2 servings

22 grams of fat

38 grams of protein

3 grams of net carbs

Ingredients

- ½ head cauliflower
- ½ cup heavy cream
- 12 oz. large shrimp, peeled
- 1 tsp. garlic powder
- ½ lemon

Instructions

1. Steam the cauliflower florets for 10 minutes.
2. Blend the florets in a blender with a ¼ cup of heavy cream. Season with salt and pepper.
3. Cook the shrimp on medium heat for 3 minutes on each side or until fully pink. Season with salt and pepper.
4. Add in the rest of the heavy cream, garlic powder and lemon juice. Cook the shrimp for another minute, stirring. Serve and enjoy!

Pepper-Crusted Flank Steak

You'll wonder why you've never broiled a steak before when you try this pepper-crusted flank steak. Crisp and juicy all in one creamy package.

Nutrition

445 calories per serving | Makes 2 servings

27 grams of fat

38 grams of protein

5 grams of net carbs

Ingredients

- 16 spears asparagus
- 12 oz. flank steak
- 6 oz. white or brown mushrooms
- 1 clove garlic
- ¼ cup heavy cream

Instructions

1. Cut the fibrous ends off the asparagus and roast at 400°F for 15 minutes.
2. Liberally season the steak with salt and pepper. Broil for 5 minutes on each side.
3. Cook the mushrooms and a clove of crushed garlic in a well-oiled pan for 8 minutes. Add in heavy cream, stir and allow to thicken.
4. Cover the steak with foil and let it rest for 5 minutes before slicing and serving together.

Ham & Cheddar Quiche

Breakfast for dinner! This hearty, crustless quiche is a great, one-pan dinner that bakes while you set the table!

Nutrition

370 calories per serving | Makes 4 servings

- 30 grams of fat
- 20 grams of protein
- 1.7 grams of net carbs

🕐 **Prep Time: 8 mins | Cook Time: 40 mins**

Ingredients

- 4 large eggs
- ½ cup heavy cream
- 1 cup shredded cheddar cheese
- 1 cup ham, cubed
- 4 stalks green onion

Instructions

1. Crack the eggs into a mixing bowl and whisk with heavy cream until pale yellow.
2. Add in cheddar, ham, chopped green onion and salt and pepper. Stir until well incorporated.
3. Add quiche batter to an oven-safe pan or a cast iron skillet. Bake at 350°F for 40 minutes.
4. Allow to cool lightly then slice and serve.

Shrimp Tartar

Our shrimp tartar dish is delightfully tasty and extremely simple to make. Serve it in a cylindrical shape to impress your guests!

Nutrition

410 calories per serving | Makes 2 servings

- 35 grams of fat
- 35 grams of protein
- 5 grams of net carbs

Ingredients

- 16 oz. large shrimp, peeled
- 1 ½ medium avocados
- 1 campari tomato
- 3 tbsp. mayonnaise
- 1 tsp. Dijon mustard

Instructions

1. Cook the shrimp in a lightly oiled pan on medium heat for about 3 minutes on each side. Add to a mixing bowl with the mayonnaise and Dijon mustard.
2. Dice the avocado and tomato and add them to the bowl as well.
3. Season with salt and pepper to taste and toss everything very well. Serve chilled and enjoy!

Lasagna Express

Lasagna with just 5 ingredients? No way! Yes way. Warning: You may start questioning if lasagna ever had pasta in it in the first place.

Nutrition

573 calories per serving | Makes 4 servings

- 46 grams of fat
- 33 grams of protein
- 5 grams of net carbs

Ingredients

- 1 lb. ground beef
- 1 cup marinara sauce
- 1 large zucchini
- 10 oz. ricotta cheese
- 4 oz. shredded mozzarella

Instructions

1. Preheat oven to 350°F. Peel the zucchini into strips using a vegetable peeler and set aside the cores. Salt the strips and let them sit for 15 minutes. After that, gently squeeze out the excess water using a clean kitchen towel.
2. Brown the ground beef in an oiled frying pan. Add marinara and season well with salt and pepper.
3. Layer into a 9x9" casserole dish: meat, cover with zucchini strips, ricotta, meat, cover with zucchini strips, ricotta, mozzarella.
4. Cover with foil and bake for 30 minutes. Then, broil uncovered for 2–3 minutes to caramelize the top.

Crispy Buffalo Wings

Who knew a classic could be so easy? If you're a fan of spicy, you'll love these simple buffalo wings!

Nutrition

725 calories per serving | Makes 2 servings

56 grams of fat	
49 grams of protein	
3 grams of net carbs	

🕐 **Prep Time: 10 mins | Cook Time: 16 mins**

Ingredients

- 6 chicken wings
- ½ cup *Frank's Red Hot sauce*
- 2 tbsp. unsalted butter
- 6 oz. cole slaw salad mix
- 2 tbsp. mayonnaise

Instructions

1. Separate the chicken wings into 6 wingettes and 6 drumettes. Season with salt and pepper.
2. On a foil-lined baking sheet, broil on high for 16 minutes flipping them all halfway through.
3. Melt *Frank's Red Hot sauce* and the butter in a pan on a very low flame. Season the sauce with salt and pepper.
4. After broiling, toss the wings in the pan with the melted sauce. Serve with a side of the cole slaw salad mixed with mayonnaise.

Tip: *Cole slaw is best served cold so make it ahead of time and chill it in the refrigerator.*

Hollandaise Salmon

Zesty and creamy! Hollandaise sauce pairs perfectly with the flavor and texture of salmon. Easier to make than you think!

Nutrition

415 calories per serving | Makes 2 servings

- 28 grams of fat
- 37 grams of protein
- 3 grams of net carbs

Ingredients

- 2 6-oz. salmon fillets
- 1 large egg yolk
- 1 tbsp. lemon juice
- 2 tbsp. unsalted butter, cubed
- 1 large zucchini

Instructions

1. Pan fry the salmon fillets for 5 minutes on each side. Set them aside after cooking.
2. Whisk the egg yolk in a double boiler until pale yellow. Add lemon juice and whisk until thickened.
3. Add a tablespoon of butter at a time until each is incorporated into the sauce. Add a teaspoon of water if the sauce becomes too thick.
4. Spiralize the zucchini into zoodles using a vegetable spiralizer. Fry the zoodles in a lightly oiled pan for no longer than 2 minutes, tossing continuously.
5. Serve everything together and enjoy!

207

Thyme Butter Basted Ribeye

Crispy on the outside, juicy on the inside and basted with thyme and butter — a classic low-carb dinner that'll impress and satisfy.

Nutrition

745 calories per serving | Makes 2 servings

- 65 grams of fat
- 32 grams of protein
- 5 grams of net carbs

⏱ **Prep Time: 4 hours | Cook Time: 30 mins**

Ingredients

- 12 oz. ribeye steak
- 2 tbsp. unsalted butter
- 2 sprigs fresh thyme
- 6 oz. Brussels sprouts
- 2 tbsp. olive oil

Instructions

1. Salt the steak liberally for 4 hours before cooking and keep in the refrigerator.
2. Toss the Brussels sprouts in olive oil and roast them for 25 minutes at 375°F.
3. Heat up an oiled skillet until very hot. Cook the steak for 4 minutes on first side (this will make a medium rare steak).
4. Flip, add butter and thyme, and baste with a spoon for another 4 minutes while frying.
5. Let the steak rest, covered, for 5 minutes and enjoy with the roasted Brussels sprouts.

Cheesy Portobello Burgers

Mushroom lovers rejoice! These Portobello burgers are a twist on traditional burgers and stuffed mushrooms and will leave you craving more!

Nutrition

675 calories per serving | Makes 2 servings

- 49 grams of fat
- 52 grams of protein
- 4 grams of net carbs

🕐 **Prep Time: 10 mins | Cook Time: 12 mins**

Ingredients

- 2 portobello mushrooms
- 12 oz. ground beef
- 4 oz. shredded cheddar cheese
- 1 oz. baby spinach
- 4 tbsp. Parmesan cheese

Instructions

1. Mince the mushroom stems and spinach and combine with beef, cheddar, salt & pepper.
2. Make two patties and press into the underside of the mushrooms.
3. Bake on a baking sheet at 375°F for 10 minutes. Sprinkle Parmesan on top & bake for 5 more minutes.

Optional: *Broil for 2 minutes to caramelize the Parmesan.*

Dessert
IN FIVE

30 *low-carb* desserts

Up to **5** net carbs, **5** ingredients & **5** easy steps for every recipe

Raspberry Danish Cookies

All your favorite things about Danishes turned into bite-sized, baked-to-perfection cookies! Sweet, tart and delightfully dense!

Nutrition

281 calories per 2 cookies | Makes 8 cookies

| 25 grams of fat
| 9 grams of protein
| 4.5 grams of net carbs

⏱ **Prep Time: 20 mins | Cook Time: 12 mins**

Ingredients

- 4 oz. cream cheese
- 1 large egg
- 6 tbsp. powdered erythritol
- 1 cup almond flour
- 1 oz. raspberries

Instructions

1. To make the dough, blend half the cream cheese, the egg, 4 tablespoons of erythritol and the almond flour with a pinch of salt.
2. To make the Danish filling, beat together the rest of the cream cheese and 1 tablespoon of erythritol in another bowl.
3. In a food processor, pulse 1 tablespoon of erythritol and the raspberries until broken down.
4. Scoop the dough onto a cookie sheet and make a well in each one. Add some of the cream cheese mixture followed by the raspberry mixture.
5. Bake for 12 minutes at 350°F, let cool and enjoy!

Sugar-Free Nutella

Yes, you read that right: sugar-free *Nutella* can be yours in only 5 ingredients! Our recipe is easy to make and is much healthier than the store-bought stuff.

Nutrition

215 calories per 2 tbsp. | Makes 1 cup

- 20 grams of fat
- 4 grams of protein
- 3 grams of net carbs

🕐 **Prep Time: 25 mins | Cook Time: 0 mins**

Ingredients

- 2 cups hazelnuts, preferably roasted
- 6 tbsp. cocoa powder
- ½ cup granular erythritol
- 1 tbsp. coconut oil
- ½ cup unsweetened almond milk

Instructions

1. Roast the hazelnuts, if not already roasted, on a baking sheet in a 350°F oven for about 5–10 minutes or until lightly browned.
2. Add the hazelnuts into a food processor and blend until they resemble nut butter.
3. Add in the cocoa powder, erythritol, coconut oil and a pinch of salt. Blend again until fully combined.
4. Add 2 tablespoons of almond milk at a time, blending between each addition. Stop when it reaches a *Nutella*-like consistency. Keep refrigerated and enjoy!

Tip: *Removing the skins off the hazelnuts after toasting will create a silkier finished product, but it's optional!*

Coconut Cream Pie

The perfect combination of crispy and crunchy paired with smooth and creamy! This coconut cream pie is everything you're dreaming of!

Nutrition

423 calories per serving | Makes 8 slices

- 44 grams of fat
- 3 grams of protein
- 5 grams of net carbs

🕐 **Prep Time: 30 mins | Cook Time: 15 mins**

Ingredients

- 200 grams unsweetened flaked coconut
- ¼ cup coconut oil
- ¾ cup powdered erythritol
- ¾ tsp. xanthan gum
- 2 cups heavy cream

Instructions

1. Blend 100 grams of the flaked coconut, coconut oil and ¼ cup erythritol. Press into an 8" round pie pan and bake for 10 minutes at 350°F.
2. Whisk xanthan gum into the heavy cream in a pot on low heat until well incorporated. Then add the powdered erythritol and 50 grams of flaked coconut. Let boil, then let sit for 10 minutes.
3. On a baking sheet, toast 50 grams of flaked coconut for 5 minutes at 350°F.
4. Pour the cream mixture onto the cooled crust.
5. Sprinkle with the toasted flaked coconut and refrigerate for at least 12 hours. Enjoy!

Cheesecake for One

Easier to make than a whole cheesecake but just as delicious! Grab these easy ingredients, some fresh strawberries and get baking.

Nutrition

140 calories per cake | Makes 2 cheesecakes

- 14 grams of fat
- 2 grams of protein
- 2 grams of net carbs

Ingredients

- 6 oz. cream cheese
- 10 drops liquid stevia
- 1 large egg
- 2 tbsp. granular erythritol
- 50 grams strawberries, sliced

Instructions

1. Whip the cream cheese, stevia and a pinch of salt with an electric hand mixer until creamy.
2. Beat an egg in a small bowl and slowly add it to the cream cheese while mixing.
3. Then, add the erythritol and mix to combine.
4. Lightly oil 2 ramekins and divide batter equally. Bake for 30 minutes at 300°F and then chill for about 4 hours or preferably overnight.
5. Top with sliced strawberries and enjoy!

Chocolate Peanut Butter Cups

Your favorite shareable candy can now be made sugar-free! Just 5 easy ingredients and you'll be ready to dig in to peanut buttery goodness.

Nutrition

350 calories per 2 cups | Makes 8 cups

- 29 grams of fat
- 10 grams of protein
- 5 grams of net carbs

⏱ **Prep Time: 20 mins | Cook Time: 0 mins**

Ingredients

- 4 oz. unsweetened baker's chocolate
- 1 tbsp. coconut oil
- 4 tbsp. powdered erythritol
- 6 tbsp. peanut butter
- 1 pinch of salt

Instructions

1. Melt the chocolate and coconut oil in a double boiler. Add 2 tablespoons of erythritol and salt and stir well to dissolve the erythritol.
2. Equally divide half the chocolate mixture among 8 silicone cupcake molds. Chill until set.
3. Melt the peanut butter in the microwave in 30 second intervals. Add 2 tablespoons of erythritol and stir.
4. Equally divide the peanut butter mixture into the molds over the hardened chocolate. Chill until set.
5. Top with the rest of the chocolate and chill until set. Remove from molds, serve and enjoy!

Crazy for Coconut Cake

This sugar-free, dairy-free coconut cake is easy to make and you won't believe how moist and delicate it turns out! A family favorite, for sure.

Nutrition

368 calories per serving | Makes 6 servings

▌ 36 grams of fat

▌ 6 grams of protein

▌ 5 grams of net carbs

Ingredients

- 2 cups canned unsweetened coconut milk
- ⅓ cup granular erythritol
- 3 large eggs
- ⅓ cup powdered erythritol
- 2 cups unsweetened shredded coconut

Instructions

1. In a pot on medium heat, mix 1 cup of coconut milk with the granular erythritol. Once at a boil, reduce to a simmer for 20 minutes, stirring occasionally.
2. Then, add this mixture to a bowl along with eggs and powdered erythritol and mix to combine well.
3. Add the shredded coconut, the remaining cup of coconut milk and a pinch of salt. Stir well.
4. Bake in a lightly oiled, 8×8″ baking dish for 40 minutes at 350°F or until golden.
5. Serve with a sprinkle of shredded coconut and enjoy!

Macadamia Nut Clusters

Sweet, chocolatey and nutty, this dessert has it all. Only 5 ingredients, minimal assembly and absolutely no baking required!

Nutrition

100 calories per cluster | Makes 10 clusters

| 9 grams of fat
| 1 gram of protein
| 1.3 grams of net carbs

⏱ **Prep Time: 20 mins | Cook Time: 0 mins**

Ingredients

- ½ cup heavy cream
- 50 grams unsweetened baker's chocolate
- 15–20 drops liquid stevia
- 10 whole pecans
- 20 macadamia nuts

Instructions

1. Heat the heavy cream on low heat (don't boil it!) and add finely chopped baker's chocolate into it. Stir until fully melted and sweeten with stevia, if desired.
2. Arrange the 1 pecan and 2 macadamias in 10 small piles on a parchment paper-lined baking sheet.
3. Pour or spoon about a teaspoon of the chocolate mixture onto each pile, covering all the nuts to ensure they all stick together.
4. Sprinkle some chopped pecans and sea salt over each cluster and refrigerate until set, about 4 hours.

Tip: Toast your nuts for deeper flavor!

Classic Crème Brûlée

You won't believe the things you can do with erythritol. It even browns and hardens like sugar! Impress everyone with this classic crème brûlée.

Nutrition

475 calories per serving | Makes 2 servings

49 grams of fat

5 grams of protein

4 grams of net carbs

Ingredients

- 4 tbsp. granular erythritol
- 1 cup heavy cream
- 2 large egg yolks
- 1 tsp. vanilla extract
- 1 pinch of salt

Instructions

1. Preheat the oven to 300°F. Add 3 tablespoons of erythritol to heavy cream in a small pot. Heat gently on a low flame until dissolved.
2. Whisk egg yolks, vanilla extract and a pinch of salt until pale and thick. Continue to whisk while SLOWLY adding in the heavy cream to the egg yolks.
3. Place 2 ramekins in a baking dish and pour hot water into the dish until halfway up the ramekins' sides.
4. Pour the crème brûlée batter into the ramekins and bake for 35 minutes.
5. Chill for at least 4 hours. Before serving, sprinkle ½ a tablespoon of erythritol per ramekin on top and broil until caramelized.

Double Chocolate Mousse

Two kinds of chocolate are better than one! Layer our double chocolate mousse into a container of your choice and enjoy its creaminess!

Nutrition

469 calories per serving | Makes 2 servings

- 45 grams of fat
- 7 grams of protein
- 5 grams of net carbs

🕐 **Prep Time: 25 mins | Cook Time: 0 mins**

Ingredients

- 1 oz. sugar-free chocolate chips
- 1 cup heavy cream
- 4 oz. cream cheese
- ¼ cup powdered erythritol
- 2 tbsp. cocoa powder

Instructions

1. Melt the chocolate chips on very low heat in a pan with ¼ cup of heavy cream.
2. In a bowl, beat the cream cheese and erythritol. Then, add in the melted chocolate chips, cocoa powder and a pinch of salt. Beat well until fully incorporated.
3. In another bowl, beat the remaining ¾ cup of heavy cream until whipped.
4. Into 2 glass serving glasses, layer: chocolate, cream, chocolate, cream and top with more chocolate chips and/or chocolate shavings.

Lemon Dream Bars

You and your guests will be left satisfied after these dense, wonderful lemon dream bars! Finish them off with lemon and a sprinkle of erythritol.

Nutrition

272 calories per serving | Makes 8 servings

| 26 grams of fat
| 8 grams of protein
| 4 grams of net carbs

🕐 **Prep Time: 20 mins | Cook Time: 45 mins**

Ingredients

- ½ cup unsalted butter, melted
- 1¾ cups almond flour
- 1 cup powdered erythritol
- 3 medium lemons
- 3 large eggs

Instructions

1. Mix butter, 1 cup almond flour, ¼ cup erythritol and a pinch of salt. Press evenly into an 8×8" parchment paper-lined baking dish. Bake for 20 minutes at 350°F. Then let cool for 10 minutes.
2. Into a bowl, zest one of the lemons, then juice all 3 lemons, add in the eggs, ¾ cup erythritol, ¾ cup almond flour and a pinch of salt. Mix well to make the bars' filling.
3. Pour the filling onto the cooled crust and bake for 25 minutes.
4. Serve with lemon slices and a sprinkle of powdered erythritol.

Avocado Chocolate Mousse

Don't knock it 'til you've tried it! Putting avocado into desserts gives them a silky, creamy texture without adding too many extra carbs!

Nutrition

290 calories per serving | Makes 2 servings

| 25 grams of fat
| 6 grams of protein
| 3 grams of net carbs

⏱ **Prep Time: 10 mins | Cook Time: 0 mins**

Ingredients

- 300 grams avocado (about 2 medium fruit)
- 6 tsp. cocoa powder
- 3 tbsp. granular erythritol
- 1 tsp. vanilla extract
- 2 tbsp. unsweetened almond milk

Instructions

1. Peel and core the 2 avocados.
2. Add them, along with the rest of the ingredients and a pinch of salt into a food processor and blend until smooth and creamy.
3. Divide into two serving dishes and enjoy!

Tip: *A pinch of cayenne pepper makes this a spiced treat and can mask the flavor of the avocado even more!*

Stracciatella Gelato

Stracciatella gelato is the Italian phrase for chocolate chip ice cream! Feel like you're in Italy for a moment with every bite (or lick).

Nutrition

440 calories per serving | Makes 4 servings

■ 43 grams of fat

■ 5 grams of protein

■ 5 grams of net carbs

Instructions

1. Add erythritol, vanilla extract and a pinch of salt to the heavy cream in a pot and heat gently until dissolved.
2. Whisk the egg yolks in a bowl. Slowly add 1–2 ladles of the hot cream while whisking to temper the eggs so they don't cook.

⏱ **Prep Time: 30 mins | Cook Time: 0 mins**

Ingredients

- ⅔ cup granular erythritol
- 1 tsp. vanilla extract
- 1¾ cups heavy cream
- 3 large egg yolks
- ⅓ cup sugar-free chocolate chips

3. Pour the egg yolk mixture into the pot and gently heat until the whole thing can coat the back of a spoon. Then let cool *completely*.
4. Pour the batter into the (frozen overnight) drum of an ice cream maker and let it churn according to instructions. Add chocolate chips in the last 5 minutes. Chill in the freezer for a minimum of 4 hours and serve!

Tip: *Add 1 tablespoon of vodka in step 3 to keep the ice cream soft after freezing.*

Almond Fudge Brownies

These almond butter brownies are full of fat and fiber. You'll love them with a scoop of your favorite low-carb ice cream!

Nutrition

153 calories per brownie | Makes 12 brownies

▌ 14 grams of fat

▌ 8 grams of protein

▌ 3 grams of net carbs

Ingredients

- 1 cup almond butter
- ¾ cup powdered erythritol
- 3 large eggs
- 10 tbsp. cocoa powder
- ½ tsp. baking powder

Instructions

1. Use a food processor to blend together the almond butter and erythritol.
2. Then, add in the eggs, cocoa powder, baking powder and a pinch of salt.
3. Transfer the batter into a greased 9×9" baking pan and smooth the top with a spatula.
4. Bake for 11 minutes at 325°F. Cool completely to firm up before cutting and enjoying.

Strawberries & Cream Pancakes

A simple twist on cream cheese pancakes makes this recipe moist and absolutely bursting with flavor! A griddle is a must with these pancakes.

⊙ **Prep Time: 15 mins | Cook Time: 10 mins**

Nutrition

180 calories per ½ recipe | Makes 6 pancakes

▌ 14 grams of fat

▌ 8.5 grams of protein

▌ 3 grams of net carbs

Ingredients

- 2 large eggs, separated
- ½ tsp. baking powder
- 50 grams strawberries, minced
- 2 oz. cream cheese
- 10 drops liquid stevia

Instructions

1. Beat the egg whites with an electric hand mixer until foamy, then add in the baking powder. Beat until stiff peaks form.
2. Beat the egg yolks, minced strawberries, 1 oz. of cream cheese and stevia until smooth and pale. Combine with the egg whites very gently. Do not deflate the stiff egg whites!
3. Cube the remaining cream cheese and gently mix it into the pancake batter.
4. Ladle ¼ cup of batter at a time onto a griddle on low heat and cook for about 5–7 minutes or until almost fully cooked.
5. *Very* gently, flip and cook for another 1–2 minutes.

Cinnamon Mug Cake

Cinnamon is a great aromatic spice to add to cakes to make it feel like a cozy autumn's day. We love it in our low-carb desserts!

Nutrition

355 calories per cake | Makes 1 cake

- 32 grams of fat
- 12 grams of protein
- 4 grams of net carbs

⏱ **Prep Time: 8 mins | Cook Time: 10 mins**

Ingredients

- ¼ cup almond flour
- 2.5 tbsp. granular erythritol
- ½ tsp. ground cinnamon
- 1 large egg
- 1 tbsp. coconut oil

Instructions

1. Combine almond flour, erythritol, cinnamon and a pinch of salt in a bowl.
2. Then, add the egg and coconut oil. Mix well.
3. Lightly oil a ramekin and add the mug cake batter. Bake at 350°F for about 10 minutes or microwave for 1 minute.
4. Enjoy with a drizzle of sugar-free maple syrup (optional, see p. 26).

Cookie Dough Mousse

Our cookie dough mousse recipe is perfect for when that hankering for cookie dough arises! It's completely egg-free, so go ahead, munch away!

Nutrition

388 calories per serving | Makes 2 servings

- 37 grams of fat
- 6 grams of protein
- 5 grams of net carbs

⏱ **Prep Time: 10 mins | Cook Time: 0 mins**

Ingredients

- 2 tbsp. unsalted butter
- 4 oz. cream cheese
- 1.5 tsp. vanilla extract
- ¼ cup powdered erythritol
- ¼ cup sugar-free chocolate chips

Instructions

1. Melt the butter on very low heat until golden brown. Do not let it burn!
2. With an electric hand mixer, beat together the cream cheese, vanilla extract, erythritol, browned butter and a pinch of salt.
3. When smooth and combined, fold in the chocolate chips with a spatula.
4. Chill for an hour and enjoy!

Creamy Coconut Fudge

Light, creamy and uber fudgy! These creamy coconut fudge bites are full of deep, chocolatey flavor with hints of coconut!

Nutrition

220 calories per 2 squares | Makes 16 squares

▌ 22 grams of fat

▌ 3 grams of protein

▌ 3 grams of net carbs

⊙ **Prep Time: 10 mins | Cook Time: 0 mins**

Ingredients

- 8 oz. cream cheese
- 8 tbsp. coconut oil
- ½ cup cocoa powder
- ½ cup granular erythritol
- ¼ cup unsweetened flaked coconut

Instructions

1. Combine cream cheese, coconut oil, cocoa powder, erythritol and a pinch of salt in a pot on medium heat. Heat and stir until all melted.
2. To get rid of any clumps and make everything extra creamy, beat the mixture with an electric hand mixer.
3. Pour the mixture into a parchment paper-lined, 8×8" baking dish and spread to flatten. Sprinkle the top with unsweetened, toasted coconut flakes.
4. Chill overnight and then cut into 16 squares. Enjoy!

Banana Pudding

Thought you could never enjoy banana in your desserts? Think again! A vial of banana extract will add some delightfully fruity flavor to recipes.

Nutrition

455 calories per serving | Makes 1 cup

| 45 grams of fat
| 3 grams of protein
| 4.5 grams of net carbs

Ingredients

- ½ cup heavy cream
- 1 large egg yolk
- 3 tbsp. powdered erythritol
- ½ tsp. xanthan gum
- ½ tsp. banana extract

Instructions

1. In a double boiler, combine the heavy cream, egg yolk and erythritol. Whisk constantly until the mixture thickens and erythritol dissolves.
2. Add the xanthan gum and whisk until thickened even more. The mixture should be able to coat the back of a spoon.
3. Add in the banana extract and a pinch of salt. Stir and transfer to a small serving dish. Cover with plastic wrap so that it touches the surface of the pudding.
4. Refrigerate for about 4 hours and enjoy!

Tip: *Try this recipe with any flavor extracts of your choice!*

Sea Salt Chocolate Truffles

These truffles were meant to please a crowd. The next time you've got a hungry family coming over, make this recipe and watch them love it!

Nutrition

110 calories per truffle | Makes 10 truffles

10 grams of fat

1.5 grams of protein

1 gram of net carbs

🕐 **Prep Time: 25 mins | Cook Time: 0 mins**

Ingredients

- ½ cup heavy cream
- 4 oz. unsweetened baker's chocolate
- 2 tbsp. unsalted butter
- ½ cup granular erythritol
- 1 tsp. sea salt flakes

Instructions

1. In a double boiler, heat the heavy cream until hot.
2. Cut the chocolate into very small pieces and add them to the hot heavy cream. Stir until melted.
3. Take the bowl off the heat and stir in the butter. Add the erythritol, stir, and refrigerate for 1 hour.
4. Using a cookie scoop, scoop 1-inch balls, rounding them with your lightly oiled hands. Place them on a parchment paper-lined plate and sprinkle each with some sea salt flakes.
5. Refrigerate until set, about 1–2 hours, then enjoy!

Double Lemon Jell-O Cake

So light and fluffy, this double lemon Jell-O cake is a dream come true! Each bite is its own little piece of heaven right in your mouth.

Nutrition

408 calories per serving | Makes 4 servings

- 41 grams of fat
- 7 grams of protein
- 4 grams of net carbs

🕐 **Prep Time: 15 mins | Cook Time: 15 mins**

Ingredients

- 100 grams pecans
- 1 tbsp. unsalted butter, melted
- 8.5 grams sugar-free lemon Jell-O
- 8 oz. cream cheese
- 2 tbsp. fresh lemon juice

Instructions

1. Make the crust by blending together the pecans, melted butter and a pinch of salt in a food processor. Do not overblend into nut butter, just until it's very finely crushed.
2. Press the crust into a 6×6" baking dish. Bake at 350°F for 15 minutes. It should be dry to the touch. After, let it cool for 15 minutes.
3. Whisk the Jell-O powder with 1 cup of boiling water, then add cream cheese and lemon juice. Whisk until smooth.
4. Pour in the Jell-O cream cheese mixture and let chill in the refrigerator overnight. Enjoy!

Matcha Soufflé

The robust flavor of matcha pairs perfectly with the light, airy texture of a soufflé. Play around with the sweetness to let more or less matcha shine.

Nutrition

88 calories per soufflé | Makes 2 soufflés

■ 8 grams of fat

■ 4 grams of protein

■ 0.5 grams of net carbs

Ingredients

- 1 large egg, separated
- ½ tsp. baking powder
- 1 tbsp. unsalted butter, melted
- 2 tbsp. powdered erythritol
- ¾ tsp. matcha powder

Instructions

1. Beat the egg white with an electric hand mixer until foamy. Add the baking powder and beat until stiff peaks form.
2. Beat the egg yolk with the melted butter, erythritol, matcha powder and a pinch of salt.
3. Very gently, fold in the egg whites into the matcha mixture egg yolk mixture.
4. Liberally grease 2 ramekins with butter and evenly divide in the soufflé batter into each.
5. Bake for 15 minutes at 325°F and serve immediately. They will begin to deflate right away so it's best to finish baking right before eating.

Key Lime Panna Cotta

An impressive dessert made with the simplest ingredients. Think of it as a deconstructed, creamy key lime pie. You'll love the fun texture!

Nutrition

445 calories per serving | Makes 4 servings

- 44 grams of fat
- 3 grams of protein
- 5 grams of net carbs

⏱ **Prep Time: 10 mins | Cook Time: 0 mins**

Ingredients

- ¼ cup granular erythritol
- 1 packet (8 grams) unflavored gelatin
- 2 cups heavy cream
- 4 key limes, zested and juiced
- ¼ cup almond meal (or almond flour)

Instructions

1. Add the erythritol and gelatin to the heavy cream in a small pot and heat gently until both are dissolved.
2. Pour in the juice and zest of the key limes (or 2 large regular limes). Add a pinch of salt as well.
3. Grease 4 ramekins (or similar containers of choice) and pour in the panna cotta batter.
4. Chill for 4–6 hours in the refrigerator or overnight.
5. Toast the almond meal in a dry pan on low heat until lightly browned. Sprinkle and serve!

Maple Pecan Cookies

Can you imagine cookies made with only 5 ingredients? We created a deliciously toasty recipe using our trusty, low-carb, high-fat favorite nut!

Nutrition

140 calories per cookie | Makes 12 cookies

- 14 grams of fat
- 2 grams of protein
- 2 grams of net carbs

Ingredients

- 2 cups whole pecans
- 2 tbsp. sugar-free maple syrup
- 10 drops liquid stevia
- ½ tsp. ground cinnamon
- 1 large egg

Instructions

1. Toast the pecans on a baking sheet at 350°F for about 8 minutes or until lightly browned.
2. Add the pecans into a food processor and blend until they start to resemble nut butter.
3. Add in the sugar-free maple syrup, liquid stevia, cinnamon, egg and a pinch of salt. Blend again to fully incorporate.
4. Shape the dough into 12 balls, flatten slightly and add a whole pecan onto each. Bake for 15 minutes at 350°F.
5. Let cool completely before enjoying.

0-Carb Gummy Candy

Gelatin is quite versatile. Playing around with the proportion of gelatin and water will give you these fun, sugar-free gummy candies!

Nutrition

9 calories per gummy | Makes 24 gummies

| 0 grams of fat
| 1 gram of protein
| 0 grams of net carbs

Ingredients

- 3 packets (24 grams) unflavored gelatin
- ¾ cup cold water
- 1 packet (8.5 grams) sugar-free lemon Jell-O
- 1 packet (8.5 grams) sugar-free cherry Jell-O
- 1 packet (8.5 grams) sugar-free lime Jell-O

Instructions

1. Add 1 packet of gelatin, ¼ cup water and one flavor of Jell-O to a small saucepan over a low heat. Stir until all granules have dissolved, about 2–5 minutes.
2. Spoon or pour the mixture into a silicone candy mold of your choice.
3. Repeat this process for the other 2 flavors.
4. Let the gummy candies cool for a few minutes and then place them in the refrigerator for about 30 minutes to set.
5. Remove them from their molds and enjoy!

Chocolate Haystack Cookies

We loved the unique texture of these chocolate haystack cookies and we think you will too! Chewy, chocolatey and delicious!

Nutrition

300 calories per cookie | Makes 6 cookies

| ▮ 30 grams of fat
| ▮ 3.5 grams of protein
| ▮ 5 grams of net carbs

Instructions

1. In a sauce pan on a medium heat, combine the heavy cream and erythritol. Once at a boil, lower the heat to a simmer and reduce until it's about half, about 15 minutes.
2. Mix the rest of the ingredients in a bowl. Then, add in the hot condensed cream and stir well.

⏱ **Prep Time: 25 mins | Cook Time: 25 mins**

Ingredients

- 1 cup heavy cream
- 3 tbsp. granular erythritol
- 75 grams unsweetened shredded coconut
- 30 grams sliced almonds
- 84 grams sugar-free chocolate chips

3. Add the dough to a muffin tin and press each cookie down slightly.
4. Bake for about 25 minutes at 325°F. Let cookies rest for at least 30 minutes before eating.

White Chocolate Cashew Clusters

Just 5 easy-to-find ingredients and you'll be enjoying this creamy, crunchy snack with tons of flavor and fat! It's worth the effort to make them.

Nutrition

72 calories per cluster | Makes 12 clusters

- 6.5 grams of fat
- 1 gram of protein
- 1.5 grams of net carbs

⏱ **Prep Time: 30 mins | Cook Time: 0 mins**

Ingredients

- 36 whole cashews
- 12 sugar-free hard caramel candies
- 50 grams cocoa butter
- 2 tbsp. powdered erythritol
- Pink sea salt to taste

Instructions

1. Toast cashews on a parchment paper-lined baking sheet at 350°F for 5–10 minutes (optional).
2. Arrange the toasted cashews in piles of 3 and add a caramel candy onto each pile. Bake until each caramel is just slightly melted over each nut.
3. Melt the cocoa butter and erythritol and then allow to cool until it's a spoonable consistency.
4. Spoon a bit of the white chocolate mixture onto each cooled cashew cluster and top with some pink salt while still wet. Cool in the refrigerator until hardened and enjoy!

Strawberry Shortcake

A classic strawberry shortcake recipe you can make in no time. We used our trusty Oopsie Roll recipe to make this recipe fun and easy.

Nutrition

308 calories per cake | Makes 2 shortcakes

	30 grams of fat
	6 grams of protein
	5 grams of net carbs

⏱ Prep Time: 20 mins | Cook Time: 25 mins

Ingredients

- 100 grams strawberries, hulled
- 3 tbsp. powdered erythritol
- 1 large egg, separated
- 1 oz. cream cheese
- ½ cup heavy cream

Instructions

1. Thinly slice the hulled strawberries and mix with 2 tbsp. erythritol in a bowl. Let soak for 30 minutes to release juices.
2. Use a hand mixer to beat the egg white until foamy. Add a pinch of salt, 1 tablespoon of erythritol and mix again until stiff peaks form.
3. Beat the egg yolk and cream cheese until smooth. Then, gently fold the egg white into the egg yolk mixture.
4. On a parchment paper-lined baking sheet, make four 3″ circles from the egg batter. Bake for 25 minutes at 300°F. Then, let cool.
5. Beat heavy cream and the rest of the erythritol for about 1 minute. Add the whipped cream to one cake layer, then sliced strawberries and repeat to make each shortcake stack.

Pumpkin Pudding

It doesn't need to be autumn for you to enjoy some pumpkin every now and then. Keep a can of pumpkin puree in your kitchen for this very recipe!

Nutrition

156 calories per serving | Makes 1 serving

- 14 grams of fat
- 2 grams of protein
- 5 grams of net carbs

Ingredients

- ½ cup unsweetened coconut cream
- 3 tbsp. canned pumpkin
- 4 tsp. granular erythritol
- ¾ tsp. pumpkin pie spice
- ⅛ tsp. xanthan gum

Instructions

1. Mix the coconut cream, canned pumpkin, erythritol, pumpkin pie spice and a pinch of salt together in a pot on medium heat.
2. While whisking continuously, add the xanthan gum slowly. Heat the pudding on medium heat for 1 minute.
3. Refrigerate for 30 minutes to let it set slightly.
4. Sprinkle pumpkin pie spice on top and serve.

Mint Chocolate Chip Ice Cream

This keto- and paleo-friendly ice cream recipe is dairy-free, sugar-free and artificial coloring-free! The green color comes from the added avocado!

Nutrition

173 calories per scoop | Makes 9 scoops

- 18 grams of fat
- 2 grams of protein
- 3 grams of net carbs

Instructions

1. Freeze your ice cream maker's drum overnight before starting this recipe.
2. In a food processor, blend the coconut milk, erythritol, avocado and ½–1 tsp. of mint extract.
3. Fold in the chocolate chips by hand.

🕐 **Prep Time: 20 mins | Cook Time: 0 mins**

Ingredients

- 20 oz. canned unsweetened coconut milk
- ⅔ cup granular erythritol
- 1 medium avocado
- ½–1 tsp. mint extract
- ½ cup sugar-free chocolate chips

4. Churn the ice cream batter according to manufacturer's instructions. Freeze overnight.
5. Let thaw for 10–15 minutes before enjoying.

Tip: *Add 1 tablespoon of vodka in step 2 to keep the ice cream soft after freezing.*

Banana Almond Muffins

These muffins are sweet enough for dessert but nutritious enough to enjoy as a breakfast too! We toast them up with a cup of coffee or tea!

Nutrition

289 calories per muffin | Makes 6 muffins

▌ 26 grams of fat

▌ 14 grams of protein

▌ 4 grams of net carbs

⏱ **Prep Time: 10 mins | Cook Time: 18 mins**

Ingredients

- 1 cup almond butter
- ⅔ cup powdered erythritol
- 3 large eggs
- ½ tsp. banana extract
- 1 tsp. baking powder

Instructions

1. Use a food processor to blend together the almond butter and erythritol.
2. Then, add in the eggs, banana extract, baking powder and a pinch of salt.
3. Pour the batter into 6 muffin tin cups lined with muffin paper liners.
4. Bake for 16–18 minutes at 325°F. Cool completely to firm up before serving.

Thank You

Our hopes are that some of these recipes will become staples in your diet making low-carb cooking more delicious and easier for you on a daily basis.

If you have questions, suggestions or any other feedback, please don't hesitate to contact us directly: hello@tasteaholics.com.

We answer emails every day and we'd love to hear from you. Each comment we receive is valuable and helps us in continuing to provide quality content.

Your direct feedback could be used to help others discover the benefits of going low-carb!

If you have a success story, please send it to us! We're always happy to hear about our readers' success.

Thank you again and we hope you have enjoyed *Keto in Five!*

— *Vicky Ushakova & Rami Abramov*

About the Authors

Vicky Ushakova and Rami Abramov co-founded Tasteaholics.com to provide an easy way to understand why the ketogenic diet is truly effective for weight loss and health management. They create recipes that are low-carb, high-fat and maximize flavor. The books in their *Keto in Five* series are wildly popular among the low-carb community due to their simplicity and efficacy.

Vicky and Rami's mission is to continue to improve their audience's health and outlook on life through diet and nutrition education. They are dedicated to helping change the detrimental nutritional guidelines in the United States and across the globe that have been plaguing millions of people over the last 40 years.

The duo travels the world to explore new cultures, cuisines and culinary techniques which they pass on through new recipes and content available on their website.

Personal Notes

Use these pages to write down any recipe notes and more delicious ideas.

References

1. Aude, Y., A. S, Agatston, F. Lopez-Jimenez, et al. "The National Cholesterol Education Program Diet vs a Diet Lower in Carbohydrates and Higher in Protein and Monounsaturated Fat: A Randomized Trial." JAMA Internal Medicine 164, no. 19 (2004): 2141–46. doi: 10.1001/archinte.164.19.2141. jamanetwork.com/journals/jamainternalmedicine/article-abstract/217514.

2. De Lau, L. M., M. Bornebroek, J. C. Witteman, A. Hofman, P. J. Koudstaal, and M. M. Breteler. "Dietary Fatty Acids and the Risk of Parkinson Disease: The Rotterdam Study." Neurology 64, no. 12 (June 2005): 2040–5. doi:10.1212/01. WNL.0000166038.67153.9F. www.ncbi.nlm.nih.gov/pubmed/15985568/.

3. Freeman, J. M., E. P. Vining, D. J. Pillas, P. L. Pyzik, J. C. Casey, and L M. Kelly. "The Efficacy of the Ketogenic Diet-1998: A Prospective Evaluation of Intervention in 150 Children." Pediatrics 102, no. 6 (December 1998): 1358–63. www.ncbi.nlm.nih.gov/pubmed/9832569/.

4. Hemingway, C, J. M. Freeman, D. J. Pillas, and P. L. Pyzik. "The Ketogenic Diet: A 3- to 6-Year Follow-up of 150 Children Enrolled Prospectively. Pediatrics 108, no. 4 (October 2001): 898–905. www.ncbi.nlm.nih.gov/pubmed/11581442/.

5. Henderson, S. T. "High Carbohydrate Diets and Alzheimer's Disease." Medical Hypotheses 62, no. 5 (2014): 689–700. doi:10.1016/j.mehy.2003.11.028. www.ncbi.nlm.nih.gov/pubmed/15082091/.

6. Neal, E.G., H. Chaffe, R. H. Schwartz, M. S. Lawson, N. Edwards, G. Fitzsimmons, A. Whitney, and J. H. Cross. "The Ketogenic Diet for the Treatment of Childhood Epilepsy: A Randomised Controlled Trial." Lancet Neurology 7, no. 6 (June 2008): 500–506. doi:10.1016/S1474-4422(08)70092-9. www.ncbi.nlm.nih.gov/pubmed/18456557.

7. Chowdhury, R., S. Warnakula, S. Kunutsor, F. Crowe, H. A. Ward, L. Johnson, et al. "Association of Dietary, Circulating, and Supplement Fatty Acids with Coronary Risk: A Systematic Review and Meta-Analysis." Annals of Internal Medicine 160 (2014): 398–406. doi:10.7326/M13-1788. annals.org/article.aspx?articleid=1846638.

8. Siri-Tarino, P. W., Q. Sun, F. B. Hu, and R. M. Krauss. "Meta-Analysis of Prospective Cohort Studies Evaluating the Association of Saturated Fat with Cardiovascular Disease." American Journal of Clinical Nutrition 91, no. 3 (March 2010): 535–46. doi:10.3945/ajcn.2009.27725. www.ncbi.nlm.nih.gov/pubmed/20071648.

9. "Prediabetes and Insulin Resistance," The National Institute of Diabetes and Digestive and Kidney Diseases. https://www.niddk.nih.gov/health-information/diabetes/types/prediabetes-insulin-resistance.

10. "National Diabetes Statistics Report," Centers for Disease Control and Prevention, 2014. http://www.cdc.gov/diabetes/pubs/statsreport14/national-diabetes-report-web.pdf.

11. Dyson, P. A., Beatty, S. and Matthews, D. R. "A low-carbohydrate diet is more effective in reducing body weight than healthy eating in both diabetic and non-diabetic subjects." Diabetic Medicine. 2007. 24: 1430–1435. http://onlinelibrary.wiley.com/doi/10.1111/j.1464-5491.2007.02290.x/full.

12. Christopher D. Gardner, PhD; Alexandre Kiazand, MD; Sofiya Alhassan, PhD; Soowon Kim, PhD; Randall S. Stafford, MD, PhD; Raymond R. Balise, PhD; Helena C. Kraemer, PhD; Abby C. King, PhD, "Comparison of the Atkins, Zone, Ornish, and LEARN Diets for Change in Weight and Related Risk Factors Among Overweight Premenopausal Women," JAMA. 2007;297(9):969-977. http://jama.jamanetwork.com/article.aspx?articleid=205916.

13. Gary D. Foster, Ph.D., Holly R. Wyatt, M.D., James O. Hill, Ph.D., Brian G. McGuckin, Ed.M., Carrie Brill, B.S., B. Selma Mohammed, M.D., Ph.D., Philippe O. Szapary, M.D., Daniel J. Rader, M.D., Joel S. Edman, D.Sc., and Samuel Klein, M.D., "A Randomized Trial of a Low-Carbohydrate Diet for Obesity – NEJM," N Engl J Med 2003; 348:2082-2090. http://www.nejm.org/doi/full/10.1056/NEJMoa022207.

14. JS Volek, MJ Sharman, AL Gómez, DA Judelson, MR Rubin, G Watson, B Sokmen, R Silvestre, DN French, and WJ Kraemer, "Comparison of Energy-restricted Very Low-carbohydrate and Low-fat Diets on Weight Loss and Body Composition in Overweight Men and Women," Nutr Metab (Lond). 2004; 1: 13. http://www.ncbi.nlm.nih.gov/pmc/articles/PMC538279/.

15. Y. Wady Aude, MD; Arthur S. Agatston, MD; Francisco Lopez-Jimenez, MD, MSc; Eric H. Lieberman, MD; Marie Almon, MS, RD; Melinda Hansen, ARNP; Gerardo Rojas, MD; Gervasio A. Lamas, MD; Charles H. Hennekens, MD, DrPH, "The National Cholesterol Education Program Diet vs a Diet Lower in Carbohydrates and Higher in Protein and Monounsaturated Fat," Arch Intern Med. 2004;164(19):2141-2146. http://archinte.jamanetwork.com/article.aspx?articleid=217514.

16. Bonnie J. Brehm, Randy J. Seeley, Stephen R. Daniels, and David A. D'Alessio, "A Randomized Trial Comparing a Very Low Carbohydrate Diet and a Calorie-Restricted Low Fat Diet on Body Weight and Cardiovascular Risk Factors in Healthy Women," The Journal of Clinical Endocrinology & Metabolism: Vol 88, No 4; January 14, 2009. http://press.endocrine.org/doi/full/10.1210/jc.2002-021480.

17. M. E. Daly, R. Paisey, R. Paisey, B. A. Millward, C. Eccles, K. Williams, S. Hammersley, K. M. MacLeod, T. J. Gale, "Short-term Effects of Severe Dietary Carbohydrate-restriction Advice in Type 2 Diabetes–a Randomized Controlled Trial," Diabetic Medicine, 2006; 23: 15–20. http://onlinelibrary.wiley.com/doi/10.1111/j.1464-5491.2005.01760.x/abstract.

18. Stephen B. Sondike, MD, Nancy Copperman, MS, RD, Marc S. Jacobson, MD, "Effects Of A Low-Carbohydrate Diet On Weight Loss And Cardiovascular Risk Factor In Overweight Adolescents," The Journal of Pediatrics: Vol 142, Issue 3: 253-258; March 2003. http://www.sciencedirect.com/science/article/pii/S0022347602402065.

19. William S. Yancy Jr., MD, MHS; Maren K. Olsen, PhD; John R. Guyton, MD; Ronna P. Bakst, RD; and Eric C. Westman, MD, MHS, "A Low-Carbohydrate, Ketogenic Diet versus a Low-Fat Diet To Treat Obesity and Hyperlipidemia: A Randomized, Controlled Trial," Ann Intern Med. 2004;140(10):769-777. http://annals.org/article.aspx?articleid=717451.

20. Grant D Brinkworth, Manny Noakes, Jonathan D Buckley, Jennifer B Keogh, and Peter M Clifton, "Long-term Effects of a Very-low-carbohydrate Weight Loss Diet Compared with an Isocaloric Low-fat Diet after 12 Mo," Am J Clin Nutr July 2009 vol. 90 no. 1 23-32. http://ajcn.nutrition.org/content/90/1/23.long.

21. H. Guldbrand, B. Dizdar, B. Bunjaku, T. Lindström, M. Bachrach-Lindström, M. Fredrikson, C. J. Östgren, F. H. Nystrom, "In Type 2 Diabetes, Randomisation to Advice to Follow a Low-carbohydrate Diet Transiently Improves Glycaemic Control Compared with Advice to Follow a Low-fat Diet Producing a Similar Weight Loss," Diabetologia (2012) 55: 2118. http://link.springer.com/article/10.1007/s00125-012-2567-4.

22. Sharon M. Nickols-Richardson, PhD, RD, , Mary Dean Coleman, PhD, RD, Joanne J. Volpe, Kathy W. Hosig, PhD, MPH, RD, "Perceived Hunger Is Lower and Weight Loss Is Greater in Overweight Premenopausal Women Consuming a Low-Carbohydrate/High-Protein vs High-Carbohydrate/Low-Fat Diet," The Journal of Pediatrics: Vol 105, Issue 9: 1433–1437; September 2005. http://www.sciencedirect.com/science/article/pii/S000282230501151X.

23. Frederick F. Samaha, M.D., Nayyar Iqbal, M.D., Prakash Seshadri, M.D., Kathryn L. Chicano, C.R.N.P., Denise A. Daily, R.D., Joyce McGrory, C.R.N.P., Terrence Williams, B.S., Monica Williams, B.S., Edward J. Gracely, Ph.D., and Linda Stern, M.D., "A Low-Carbohydrate as Compared with a Low-Fat Diet in Severe Obesity, " N Engl J Med 2003; 348:2074-2081. http://www.nejm.org/doi/full/10.1056/NEJMoa022637.

24. Yancy WS Jr, Westman EC, McDuffie JR, Grambow SC, Jeffreys AS, Bolton J, Chalecki A, Oddone EZ, "A randomized trial of a low-carbohydrate diet vs orlistat plus a low-fat diet for weight loss," Arch Intern Med. 2010 Jan 25;170(2):136-45. http://www.ncbi.nlm.nih.gov/pubmed/20101008?itool=EntrezSystem2.PEntrez.Pubmed.Pubmed_ResultsPanel.Pubmed_RVDocSum&ordinalpos=2.

25. Swasti Tiwari, Shahla Riazi, and Carolyn A. Ecelbarger, "Insulin's Impact on Renal Sodium Transport and Blood Pressure in Health, Obesity, and Diabetes," American Journal of Physiology vol. 293, no. 4 (October 2, 2007): 974–984, http://ajprenal.physiology.org/content/293/4/F974.full.

Made in the USA
Lexington, KY
14 July 2018